HATCHMENTS IN BRITAIN

4

Bedfordshire, Berkshire, Buckinghamshire, Oxfordshire and Wiltshire

HATCHMENTS IN BRITAIN

4

Bedfordshire, Berkshire, Buckinghamshire, Oxfordshire and Wiltshire

Edited by

PETER SUMMERS, F.S.A.

PHILLIMORE

1983

Published by
PHILLIMORE & CO. LTD.
London and Chichester

Head Office: Shopwyke Hall,
Chichester, Sussex, England

© Peter Summers, 1983

ISBN 0 85033 451 9

Printed and bound in Great Britain by
THE CAMELOT PRESS LTD.
Southampton, Hants.

CONTENTS

General Introduction	ix
Abbreviations	xv
Bedfordshire	1
Berkshire	23
Buckinghamshire	41
Oxfordshire	85
Wiltshire	113
Select Bibliography	155
Index	157

ILLUSTRATIONS

BEDFORDSHIRE
Bletsoe 4: For St Andrew Beauchamp, 14th Baron St John, 1874   2

BERKSHIRE
Avington: For William James, 1666   24

BUCKINGHAMSHIRE
Stoke Poges 10: For Granville Penn, 1844   42

OXFORDSHIRE
Ashmolean Museum, Oxford: Reputed to be for John Tradescant, 1662   86

WILTSHIRE
Boyton: For H.R.H. Prince Leopold, Duke of Albany, 1884 ..   114

GENERAL INTRODUCTION

Hatchments are a familiar sight to all those who visit our parish churches. They are not only decorative, but of great interest to the herald, genealogist and local historian. It is therefore surprising that — apart from local surveys in a few counties mostly in recent years — no attempt has yet been made to record them on a national scale. This series will, it is hoped, remedy the deficiency; it is proposed to publish separate volumes covering all English counties as well as Wales, Scotland and Ireland.

It is probable that no volume will be complete. Previously unrecorded hatchments will turn up from time to time; many have already been found in obscure places such as locked cupboards and ringing chambers. There are likely to be some inaccuracies, for hatchments are often hung high up in dark corners, and the colours may have faded or be darkened with age and grime. Identification is a problem if the arms do not appear anywhere in print: and even if the arms are identified, pedigrees of the family may not always be available. But enough has been done to make publication worth while; the margin to the pages will perhaps allow for pencilled amendments and notes.

Since I began the survey in 1952 many hatchments, probably evicted at the time of Victorian restorations, have been replaced in the churches whence they came. On the other hand, during the same period just as many hatchments have been destroyed. An excuse often made by incumbents is that they are too far gone to repair, or that the cost of restoration is too great. Neither reason is valid. If any incumbent, or anyone who has the responsibility for the care of hatchments which need attention, will write to me, I shall be happy to tell him how the hatchments may be simply and satisfactorily restored at a minimal cost. It is hoped that the publication of this survey will help to draw attention to the importance of these heraldic records.

The diamond-shaped hatchment, which originated in the Low Countries, is a debased form of the medieval achievement — the shield, helm, and other accoutrements carried at the funeral of a noble or knight. In this country it was customary for the hatchment to be hung outside the house during the period of mourning, and thereafter be placed in the church. This practice, begun in the early 17th century, is by no means entirely obsolete, for about 80 examples have so far been recorded for the present century.

Closely allied to the diamond hatchment, and contemporary with the earlier examples, are rectangular wooden panels bearing coats of arms. As some of these bear no inscriptions and a black/white or white/black background, and as some otherwise typical hatchments bear anything from initials and a date to a long inscription beginning 'Near here lies buried . . .', it will be appreciated that it is not always easy to draw a firm line between the true hatchment and the memorial panel. Any transitional types will therefore also be listed, but armorial boards which are clearly intended as simple memorials will receive only a brief note.

With hatchments the background is of unique significance, making it possible to tell at a glance whether it is for a bachelor or spinster, husband or wife, widower or widow. These different forms all appear on the plate immediately following this introduction.

Royal Arms can easily be mistaken for hatchments, especially in the West Country where they are frequently of diamond shape and with a black background. But such examples often bear a date, which proves that they were not intended as hatchments. Royal hatchments, however, do exist, and any examples known will be included.

All hatchments are in the parish church unless otherwise stated, but by no means are they all in churches; many are in secular buildings and these, if they have no links with the parish in which they are now found, are listed at the end of the text. All hatchments recorded since the survey began are listed, including those which are now missing.

With only a very few exceptions all the hatchments in this volume were originally recorded by me in the 1950s; most of them I checked in the 1970s, but a great deal of re-checking has been done in the past six months by many friends, who have also given invaluable help in identification. I had intended to name, as in the previous volumes, all those who have helped since 1952 when I first started recording the hatchments in these five counties. But I have come to the conclusion that this is not practicable, as they are so many. I can only acknowledge with gratitude the splendid assistance I have received during the past thirty years. Without this help, especially in the final stages, I am sure the book would not have been ready for publication this year. I must, however, mention one of these kind friends, John Titterton, a near neighbour, who has agreed to assist me in the Editorship, and to take over from me if and when the need arises.

The illustrations on the following two pages are the work of the late Mr. G. A. Harrison and will provide a valuable 'key' for those unfamiliar with the complexity of hatchment backgrounds.

One last, but important note. Every copy sold of this book helps a child in the Third World; for I have irrevocably assigned all royalties on the entire series to a Charity, The Ockenden Venture.

PETER SUMMERS
Day's Cottage, North Stoke, Oxford

1. MARRIED MAN
2. MARRIED WOMAN
3. BACHELOR
4. WIDOW
5. WIDOWER
6. SPINSTER

1, 2, 3 and 4—
   FOR A MAN SURVIVING TWO WIVES
5. FOR A BISHOP
6. FOR A PEER OF THE REALM

ABBREVIATIONS

B.P.	=	Burke's *Peerage, Baronetage and Knightage*
B.L.G.	=	Burke's *Landed Gentry*
B.E.P.	=	Burke's *Extinct and Dormant Peerages*
B.E.B.	=	Burke's *Extinct and Dormant Baronetcies*
V.C.H.	=	*Victoria County History*
D.N.B.	=	*Dictionary of National Biography*
Lipscombe	=	Lipscombe's *History of the County of Buckingham*

NOTE

Blazons throughout are exactly as noted at the time of recording, not as they ought to be.

BEDFORDSHIRE

by

Peter Summers

Bletsoe 4: For St Andrew Beauchamp, 14th Baron St John, 1874
(*Photograph by Mr. R. L. Piron*)

INTRODUCTION

The hatchments of Bedfordshire are on the whole a dull lot, and show few interesting features. Of the total of seventy-five which have been recorded there are few early examples, the earliest probably being for John Harvey, at Northill, who died in 1692. The latest is undoubtedly for Edith St John, wife of George, 1st Baron Luke; she died in 1941. The most interesting and consistent feature of the Bedfordshire hatchments is that they are restricted to one family in so many of the parishes, the largest number in any one church being the thirteen for members of the Monoux family at Wootton. Other examples are the six Inglis hatchments at Milton Bryan, the five Thornton hatchments at Blunham and the five Harvey hatchments at Northill. At Husborne Crawley all three are for members of the Orlebar family, as are five out of the six at Podington. The most unusual arms are probably those of Hussey, which appear on the hatchment of the 14th Baron St John at Bletsoe. The blazon starts 'Quarterly per a cross of pearls or and gules' and includes an Augmentation of Honour of 'a roundel argent charged with a Turban of an Omrah of the Moghul Empire', which was granted to Lady St John's father, Admiral Sir Richard Hussey.

A hatchment at Houghton Regis bears the Brandreth arms on a lozenge, and the lozenge is surmounted by a skull. A skull in this position is said to denote the last of the family, but as the hatchment has not been firmly identified we cannot tell whether Miss Brandreth really was the last of the line.

One hatchment, formerly at Elstow, is now in the county museum, a very much more satisfactory resting place for unwanted hatchments than the bonfire to which many, though not in Bedfordshire, have in the editor's experience been consigned. Only one other hatchment in the county is not in the parish church, and that is for Lady Charlotte Russell at Woburn Abbey; there is also a hatchment for Lady Charlotte in the Russell chapel at Chenies in Buckinghamshire.

As the old county boundaries are used throughout, the seven hatchments at Everton will appear in the volume which includes Huntingdonshire.

Peter Summers

BEDFORD Museum

1. All black background
On a lozenge   Qly, 1st and 4th, Argent on a bend sable three horseshoes argent (Farrer), 2nd and 3rd, Argent on a chevron sable three bulls' heads cabossed argent (Hillersdon)   Motto: Sans Dieu rien
Probably for Sarah, 3rd dau. of Dennis Farrer-Hillersdon, d. 11 Jan. 1811, aged 64.   (M.I. at Elstow)
(This hatchment was formerly in the parish church at Elstow)

BLETSOE

1. Dexter background black
Argent on a chief gules two molets pierced or (St John)   In pretence: Azure a chevron or between in chief two roses argent barbed and seeded proper and in base a cock argent combed and wattled gules (Simond)   Baron's coronet   Crest: On a mount vert an eagle wings elevated and inverted or ducally gorged gules   Mantling: Gules and argent   Motto: Data fata secutus   Supporters: Two monkeys proper   Skull below
For John, 11th Baron St John, who m. 1755, Susannah Louisa (d. 17 Oct. 1805), dau. and co-heiress of Peter Simond, and d. 27 Apr. 1767.   (B.P. 1949 ed.)

2. All black background
St John arms only
Crest: On a mount vert an eagle wings elevated and inverted or   Mantling and motto: As 1.   Skull below and a cherub's head at each top corner of shield
Probably for William Henry Beauchamp St John, son and heir of Henry Beauchamp, 12th Baron St John of Bletsoe, who d.v.p. March 1791, aged 7. (Complete Peerage: par. regs)

3. Dexter background black
St John, in fess point the Badge of Ulster, impaling, Qly, 1st and 4th, Argent on a chevron between three cross crosslets fitchy sable three stags' heads cabossed or, on a chief gules a goat passant or (Boughton), 2nd, Sable two bars engrailed argent (Rouse), 3rd, Sable three crescents or (Boughton)   Baron's coronet   Crest and motto: As 2.   Supporters: As 1.

All, except crest, on a mantle gules and ermine
For St Andrew, 13th Baron St John, who m. 1807, Louisa, eldest dau.
of Sir Charles William Rouse-Boughton, Bt., and d. 15 Oct. 1817.
(B.P. 1949 ed.)

4. Dexter background black
St John, in fess point the Badge of Ulster, impaling, Qly per a cross of pearls or and gules in the 1st and 4th quarters a cross azure, in the 2nd and 3rd quarters three lions passant guardant, two and one or, on the centre chief point of shield, as an honourable augmentation, a roundel argent charged with a turban of an Omrah of the Moghul Empire proper (Hussey)
Baron's coronet   Crest and motto: As 1.   Supporters: Two monkeys proper each with a gold collar round the waist
For St Andrew Beauchamp, 14th Baron St John, who m. 1838, Eleanor, dau. of Vice-Adm. Sir Richard Hussey Hussey, and d. 27 Jan. 1874.   (B.P. 1949 ed.)

BLUNHAM

1. Dexter background black
Argent a chevron sable between nine thorn trees, three, three and three proper (Thornton)   In pretence: Per fess azure and gules a fess or, in chief two demi-cubit arms fesswise vested gules cuffed argent the hands proper supporting a chalice or (Godin)
Crest: Out of a ducal coronet or a lion's head sable   Mantling: Gules and argent   Motto: Resurgam
For Godfrey Thornton, who m. Jane, dau. and co-heir of Stephen Peter Godin, and d. 15 Nov. 1805, aged 68.   (B.L.G. 2nd ed.; M.I.)

2. All black background
On a lozenge surmounted by a cherub's head
Thornton   In pretence: Godin
Motto: Resurgam
For Jane, widow of Godfrey Thornton. She d. 15 Mar. 1811, aged 67.
(B.L.G. 2nd ed.; M.I.)

3. All black background
Qly, 1st and 4th, Argent a chevron sable between three thorn trees proper (Thornton), 2nd and 3rd, Per fess azure and gules a fess argent in chief a chalice or (Godin), impaling, Ermine a lion passant gules, on a chief azure three cross crosslets or (Littledale)
Crest: A lion's head erased proper ducally gorged or   Mantling: Gules and argent   Motto: Fide et virtute

Bedfordshire   7

For Stephen Thornton, who m. Mary, dau. of Thomas Littledale, and
d. 26 Aug. 1850, aged 83.   She d. 23 May 1846.   (B.L.G.
2nd ed.; M.I.)

4. Sinister background black
Qly, 1st and 4th, Thornton, as 3., 2nd and 3rd, Godin, as 1., impaling,
Gules on a bend between six roundels argent three roundels gules, a
chief or ermined sable (Dixon)
Motto: Resurgam   Shield suspended from lover's knot and
cherubs' heads at corners
For Susanna, dau. of John Dixon, of Cecil Lodge, Herts, who m. 1821,
as his 1st wife, her cousin, Godfrey Thornton, and d. 21 Feb. 1824.
(B.L.G. 2nd ed.; M.I.)

5. All black background
Qly, 1st and 4th, Thornton, as 3., 2nd and 3rd, Per fess azure and gules
a fess or in chief a quatrefoil argent (Godin), impaling, Argent on a
fess couped sable between three doves proper three annulets or (Pearse)
Crest: A lion's head erased sable ducally gorged or   Mantling:
Gules and argent
For Godfrey Thornton, who m. 2nd, Sophia, dau. of Brise Pearse, and
d. 8 Mar. 1857, aged 61.   (B.L.G. 2nd ed.; M.I.)

6. Sinister background black
Qly, 1st and 4th, Thornton, as 3., 2nd and 3rd, Godin, as 1., but fess
or, impaling, Or a chevron cotised between three demi-griffins those
in chief respectant sable (Smith)
Motto: In coelo quies
For Frances Ann, dau. of Samuel Smith, who m. Claude George
Thornton, and d. 22 Feb. 1862, aged 76.   He d. 4 Aug. 1866,
aged 90.   (M.I.)

BOLNHURST

1. All black background
On a lozenge   Gules on a bend argent three trefoils slipped vert
(Harvey), impaling, Argent on a bend engrailed azure three fleurs-de-lys
argent (Paris)
For Harriet Mary, dau. of Archibald Paris, who m. John Harvey, and d.
13 Apr. 1884. Their son, the Rev. Frederick Mortimer Harvey, was
Rector of Bolnhurst.   (B.L.G. of Ireland, 1912; Crisp's
Visitations, Vol. 2)

CAMPTON

1. Dexter background black
Argent a bend between two lions rampant sable, in chief the Badge of Ulster (Osborn), impaling, Argent a chevron between three griffins passant sable (Finch)
Crest: A lion's head erased argent ducally crowned or   Mantle: Gules and argent   Motto: Quantum in rebus inane   Supporters: Two griffins argent gutty, winged, eared and armed gules, pendent from a chain round the neck a portcullis sable   Two swords in saltire behind shield
For Sir George Osborn, 4th Bt., who m. 2nd, 1788, Heneage, dau. of Daniel, 8th Earl of Winchilsea, and d. 29 June 1818.   (B.P. 1949 ed.)

2. All black background
On an asymmetrical lozenge surmounted by two cherubs' heads
Arms: As 1.   Motto and supporters: As 1.
For Heneage, widow of Sir George Osborn, 4th Bt. She d. 4 May 1820. (B.P. 1949 ed.)

3. Dexter background black
Osborn, in dexter chief the Badge of Ulster, impaling, Argent on a bend gules three martlets or winged vert (Davers)
Crest, mantling and motto: As 1.
For Sir John Osborn, 5th Bt., who m. 1809, Frederica Louisa (d. 23 July 1870), natural dau. of Sir Charles Davers, 6th Bt., and d. 28 Aug. 1848.   (B.P. 1949 ed.)

COPLE

1. All black background
Qly, 1st and 4th, Argent a bugle stringed sable knotted or (Luke), 2nd and 3rd, Gules a fleur-de-lys argent (Launcelyn)
Crest: A bull's head couped at the shoulders sable armed and winged or   Mantling: Gules and argent   Motto: Mors janua vitæ
Unidentified

CRANFIELD

1. Dexter background black
Argent a lion rampant double-queued between three pierced molets of six points azure (Harter)   In pretence: Argent three bearded men's heads in profile sable a bordure azure (Beard)
Crest: A stag salient in a fern brake proper   Mantling: Azure and argent   Motto: Deo omnia

Bedfordshire

For the Rev. George Gardner Harter, Rector of Cranfield, who m. Elizabeth Jassy, only dau. of the Rev. James Beard, and d. 7 Feb. 1872. (M.I.)

ELSTOW

1. Dexter background black
Qly, 1st and 4th, Argent on a bend sable three horseshoes argent (Farrer), 2nd and 3rd, Argent on a chevron sable three bulls' heads cabossed argent (Hillersdon), impaling, Gules a sword in bend argent hilted or (Gee) Crest: A horseshoe argent between two wings sable Mantling: Gules and argent Motto: Sans Dieu rien
For Denis Farrer-Hillersdon, son of Elizabeth Hillersdon of Elstow and Denis Farrer of Cold Brayfield, Bucks, who m. 2nd, Sarah, dau. of Osgood Gee, of Beckenham, Kent, and d. 18 Mar. 1787. (M.I.)

2. All black background
On a lozenge surmounted by a cherub's head
Qly, 1st and 4th, Farrer, 2nd and 3rd, Argent on a fess sable three bulls' heads cabossed argent armed or (Hillersdon), impaling, Gee
Motto: Sans Dieu rien
For Sarah, widow of Denis Farrer-Hillersdon, d. 12 Jan. 1791. (M.I.)

3. All black background
On a lozenge Argent a saltire engrailed sable (Colquhoun) In pretence: Qly, 1st and 4th, Farrer, 2nd and 3rd, Hillersdon, as 1.
Motto: In coelo quies
For Elizabeth, dau. of Denis Farrer-Hillersdon, who m. William Colquhoun, and d. 20 Apr. 1841, aged 73. (Warren Dawson; M.I.)

HOUGHTON REGIS

1. Dexter background black
Qly, 1st and 4th, Per pale and per chevron argent and sable two chevrons engrailed between three escallops counterchanged (Brandreth), 2nd and 3rd, Gules on a bend argent between two spurs or leathered argent a dexter mailed cubit arm the hand holding a tilting spear proper (Gibbs), impaling, Qly, 1st, Argent three demi-savages each holding a club between nine cross crosslets three, three and three sable (Smith), 2nd Argent three saddles sable (Hervey), 3rd, Argent two bars gules charged with three roses two and one argent (Orlebar), 4th Argent on a bend sable three cross crosslets argent (Chernock), and to sinister, as for a further impalement, but probably intended as a 5th quartering, Gules a fess compony argent and sable between six cross crosslets argent (Butler)

Crests: Dexter, A dagger erect point downwards proper in front of an escallop argent   Sinister, A gauntlet in fess proper surmounted by a molet pierced or   Mantling: Gules and argent   Motto: Nunquam non paratus   Inscribed on frame: Humphrey Brandreth, Esquire.
Born July 17th 1807 died April 7th, 1864.
For Humphrey Brandreth, of Houghton House, who m. 1851, Emma Jemima Barbara, youngest dau. of Col. Charles Hervey Smith, and d. 7 Apr. 1864.   (B.L.G. 5th ed.; inscr. on hatchment frame)

2. All black background
On a lozenge surmounted by a skull
Per pale argent and sable a chevron between three escallops counterchanged (Brandreth)
Possibly for Alice Brandreth, d. unm. 1772, aged 88.   (Ped. Bed. Record Office)

HUSBORNE CRAWLEY

1. Dexter background black
Argent two bars gules charged with three roses two and one argent (Orlebar)   In pretence: Sable three scaling ladders bendwise argent (Shipton)   Crest: A demi-eagle rising argent the neck charged with a bar gemel gules   Mantling: Gules and argent   Motto: Mors janua vitæ est
For Robert Charles Orlebar, who m. Charlotte Shipton, and d. 1 Nov. 1837, aged 54.   (B.L.G. 1937 ed.; M.I.)

2. All black background
On a lozenge   Orlebar   In pretence: Sable three scaling ladders bendwise in bend sinister argent (Shipton)
For Charlotte, widow of Robert Charles Orlebar. She d. 17 Dec. 1837, aged 55.   (B.L.G. 1937 ed.; M.I.)

3. All black background
Orlebar   In pretence: Azure three eels naiant fesswise in pale argent (Ellis)   Crest: As 1.   Motto: Vix ea nostra voco
For Robert Shipton Orlebar, of Crawley House, who m. 1834, Charlotte, dau. of the Rev. Valentine Ellis, and d. 8 Jan. 1879. She d. 3 Jan. 1905.   (B.L.G. 1937 ed.)

KEMPSTON

1. All black background
Sable a lion rampant between eight cross crosslets argent (Long)

Bedfordshire   11

Crest: Out of a ducal coronet or a demi-lion argent   Mantling:
Gules and argent   Motto: Resurgam
For Sir William Long, d. 2 Nov. 1841, aged 84.   (M.I.)

MARSTON MORTEYNE

1. Dexter background black
Azure standing on a base argent three naked savages proper girt about
the loins vert, each holding in the dexter hand a club over the left
shoulder proper (Wood), impaling, Azure on a bend argent between two
leopards' faces or a crown between two fleurs-de-lys or (Bromhead)
Crest: On a mount vert a tree proper fructed or   No mantling or
motto
For the Rev. James Wood, D.D., Rector of Marston Morteyne for 19
years, who m. Frances, dau. of Lt.-Col. Boardman Bromhead, and
d. 26 Dec. 1814, aged 64. She d. 8 Feb. 1842, aged 79.   (M.I.)

MILTON BRYAN

1. Sinister background black
Azure a lion rampant within a bordure argent, on a chief or three
molets of six points azure (Inglis)   In pretence: Argent on a pile
azure three ounces' heads erased or (Johnson)
Motto: Rest in heaven   Shield suspended from a bow of blue ribbons
and with a cherub's head at each top corner of shield
For Catherine, dau. and co-heir of Harry Johnson, who m. 1784, as
his 1st wife, Hugh Inglis, and d. 1 May 1792.   (B.P. 1855 ed.; M.I.)

2. Dexter background black
Qly, 1st and 4th, Azure a lion rampant argent, on a chief or three
molets of six points azure (Inglis), 2nd and 3rd, Argent a chevron
between three powets and a bordure sable (Russell), in centre chief
the Badge of Ulster   Two escutcheons of pretence: Dexter, Qly, 1st,
Argent on a pile azure three ounces' heads erased argent (Johnson),
2nd, Argent on a chevron azure, between three roundels sable each
charged with a woolsack argent, three garbs or (Wolsey), 3rd, Argent a
chevron between three lions' heads erased sable crowned or (Johnson),
4th, Gules a cross crosslet crossed or (?Chadderton)
Sinister, Qly, 1st and 4th, Sable a wolf rampant and in chief three
molets of six points or (Wilson), 2nd and 3rd, Sable a chevron between
three stags' attires argent (Cocks)
Crest: A demi-lion proper holding in dexter paw a molet or six points
or   Mottoes: (over crest) Nobilis est ira leonis   (below arms) Recte
faciendo securus   Supporters: Dexter, A leopard proper   Sinister,
A lion proper   All on a mantle gules and ermine

12   Bedfordshire

For Sir Hugh Inglis, 1st Bt. (cr. 1801), who m. 1st, Catherine, dau. and co-heir of Harry Johnson, and 2nd, Mary, dau. and heir of George Wilson, and d. 21 Aug. 1820. (Sources, as 1.)

3. All black background
On a lozenge   Qly, 1st, Azure a lion rampant or, on a chief or three molets of six points azure, in chief the Badge of Ulster (Inglis), 2nd and 3rd, Argent a chevron between three powets sable (Russell), 4th, as 1st but no Badge of Ulster   In pretence: As sinister of 2.
No motto   Supporters: As 2.
For Mary, 2nd wife of Sir Hugh Inglis, 1st Bt. She d. 23 Aug. 1835. (Sources, as 1).

4. Dexter background black
Qly, 1st and 4th, Azure a lion rampant within a bordure argent, on a chief or three estoiles of six points azure (Inglis), 2nd, Russell, as 2., 3rd, qly. i & iv. Argent on a pile azure three ounces' heads erased argent (Johnson), ii. & iii. Argent a chevron sable between three lions' heads couped gules crowned or (Johnson), over all the Badge or Ulster, impaling, Argent three greyhounds courant in pale sable (Biscoe)
Crest: As 2.   Mantling (slight): Azure and or   Mottoes and supporters: As 2. (On back of canvas: R. Walker, 20 Princes Street, Leicester Square, 1855).
For Sir Robert Harry Inglis, 2nd Bt., who m. 1807, Mary, only child of Joseph Seymour Biscoe, and d. 5 May 1855.   (Sources, as 1.)

5. All black background
On a lozenge suspended from a bow of blue ribbon
Arms: As 4.
Supporters: As 2.
For Mary, widow of Sir Robert Harry Inglis, 2nd Bt.   She d. 12 Oct. 1872. (Sources, as 1.)

6. All black background
On a lozenge surmounted by decorative scrollwork, and surmounted by a cherub's head   Qly, 1st and 4th, Inglis, as 4th of 3., 2nd, Russell, as 2., 3rd, Argent on a pile azure three ounces' heads erased argent (Johnson)
(On back of canvas: RM 132 Prepared by Roberson and Miller, 51 Long Acre, London)
Probably for either Stephena Anne Inglis, eldest dau. of Sir Hugh Inglis, 1st Bt., who d. 25 Apr. 1839; or for her younger sister, Mary Louisa Inglis, who d. 20 Oct. 1853. (Sources, as 1.)

(These six hatchments, when recorded in May 1982, were in varying degrees of decay, and need urgent attention; until they are restored they cannot be rehung)

Bedfordshire

NORTHILL

1. All black background
On a lozenge surmounted by a cherub's head   Gules on a chevron between three leopards' faces or three trefoils slipped vert (Harvey), impaling, Qly, 1st and 4th, Qly embattled gules and or in the first quarter a tower argent surmounted by a lion statant guardant or (Robinson), 2nd and 3rd, Vert a stag trippant within an orle of trefoils slipped or (Robinson)
For Sarah Gore, dau. of Sir John Robinson, 2nd Bt., who m. John Harvey, and d. 1760. He d. 17 Nov. 1721, aged 54. (B.L.G. 1937 ed.; M.I.; Romney Sedgwick, The House of Commons, 1717-1754)

2. Dexter background black
Or on a chevron gules between three leopards' faces proper three trefoils slipped argent (Harvey), impaling, Argent a chevron sable between three bombs fired proper (Silcock)
Crest: A leopard passant proper in the dexter paw a trefoil slipped sable   Mantling: Gules and argent   Motto: Vivit post funera virtus
Inscribed in bottom angle: July 22nd 1793
For John Harvey, who m. Sarah Silcock, and d. 22 July 1793.
(B.L.G. 1937 ed.; inscr. on hatchment)

3. Dexter background black
Harvey, as 2., impaling, Qly, 1st and 4th, Chequy argent and gules, 2nd and 3rd, Ermine; all within a bordure engrailed qly ermine and gules (Gibbard)
Crest and mantling: As 2.
For John Harvey, who m. Susannah, youngest dau. of John Gibbard, of Sharnbrook, and d. 20 June 1819. She d. 12 Jan. 1820.
(B.L.G. 1937 ed; M.I.)

4. All black background
Harvey, as 2., but leopards' faces gules   In pretence: Argent three cocks gules (Cockayne)
Crest: A leopard passant proper collared and corded or in the dexter paw a trefoil slipped sable   Mantling: Gules and argent   Motto: In coelo quies   Skull in base
For John Harvey, who m. Beatrice Cockayne, of Cockayne Hatley, and d. 17 Sept. 1771. (B.L.G. 2nd ed.; Gents. Mag. 426)

5. Dexter background black
Harvey, as 2., but trefoils or, impaling, Argent on a bend sable three mascles argent ( )   Crest: not discernible   Mantling: Gules and argent   Motto: Mors janua vitæ
Probably for John Harvey, of Ickwellbury, who m. Mary, widow of John Vassall, of Hoxton, and d. 1692.   (V.C.H., ii. 242)

ODELL

1. Dexter background black
Azure ten estoiles four, three, two, one or, in centre chief the Badge of Ulster (Alston), impaling, Sable three rams' heads cabossed argent (Durnford)   Crest: Between the horns of a crescent argent an estoile of six points or   Mantling: Gules and argent   Motto: In coelo quies   Two cherubs' heads flanking shield
For Sir Rowland Alston, 6th Bt., who m. Gertrude, sister of Stillingfleet Durnford, and d.s.p. 29 June 1790, aged 64.   (B.E.B.)

2. All black background
On a lozenge surmounted by a cherub's head
Arms: As 1.
Motto: Resurgam
For Gertrude, widow of Sir Rowland Alston, 6th Bt.   She d. 13 Mar. 1807.   (B.E.B.; Complete Baronetage)

3. Dexter background black
Alston, no Badge of Ulster, impaling, Argent a cross sable (Raynsford)
Crest, mantling and motto: As 1.
For Thomas Alston, who succeeded to the family estates on the death of his uncle, Sir Rowland Alston, 6th and last Bt.   He m. Elizabeth Raynesford, of Brixworth Hall, Northants, and d. 31 Jan. 1823. (B.E.B.; Gents Mag. 189)

4. Sinister background black
Argent on a saltire engrailed sable between four daggers points downwards gules a sun in splendour or, on a chief gules three cushions or (Johnston), impaling, Argent on a chief gules two molets or (St John)   Shield surmounted by a cherub's head
For Edith Laura, 5th dau. of Beauchamp, 16th Baron St John, who m. 1902, George, 1st Baron Luke, and d. 2 Aug. 1941. He d. 23 Feb. 1943.   (B.P. 1949 ed.)

PODINGTON

1. All black background
On a lozenge   Argent two bars gules charged with three roses two and one argent (Orlebar), impaling, Sable a fess and in chief three mascles argent (Powney)
Motto: In morte quies
For Elizabeth Powney, of Braywick, Berks, who m. 1687, Cooper Orlebar, and was buried 11 Feb. 1718.   He d. 1689, aged 29. (B.L.G. 2nd ed.)

Bedfordshire

2. Sinister background black
Orlebar, impaling, Argent on a bend sable three dolphins embowed argent (Rolt)
Crest: An eagle's head between two wings erect argent the neck charged with a collar gemel gules   Mantling: Gules and argent   Motto: Melior pars vivit
For Mary, dau. of Samuel Rolt, M.P., of Milton Ernest, who m. 1729, John Orlebar, and d. 23 June 1762.   (B.L.G. 1937 ed.; M.I.)

3. All black background
Orlebar arms only
Crest and mantling: As 2.   Motto: The path to happier life
Inscribed in top angle: John Orlebar, Esq. died Dec. 19th, 1765.
For John Orlebar, who m. 1729, Mary, dau. of Samuel Rolt, and d. 19 Dec. 1765.   (B.L.G. 1937 ed.)

4. Dexter background black
Orlebar, impaling, Argent on a fess gules three cross crosslets argent (Cuthbert)
Crest and mantling: As 2.   Motto: Our redeemer liveth   Skull and crossbones below
Inscribed on frame: Richard Orlebar, Esq. died Nov. 9th 1803, aged 67.
For Richard Orlebar, who m. 1767, as his 1st wife, Elizabeth, dau. of the Rev. Joseph Cuthbert, Rector of Bulpham, Essex, and d. 9 Nov. 1803, aged 67.   (B.L.G. 1937 ed.; M.I.)

5. Dexter background black
Qly, 1st, Orlebar, 2nd, Azure on two bars or three cross crosslets fitchy two and one gules, on a chief argent three escallops gules (Dilley), 3rd, Gules a chevron engrailed ermine between three eagles close proper, a crescent for difference (Child), 4th, Sable on a chevron or between three bezants three fleurs-de-lys sable, a crescent for difference (Payne)   In pretence: Azure a fess and in chief three leopards' faces or (Longuet)
Crest and mantling: As 2.   Motto: Resurgam
Inscribed on frame: Richard Orlebar, Esq. died Jan. 20th 1833, aged 57.
For Richard Orlebar, J.P., D.L., who m. 1804, Maria, dau. of Benjamin Longuet, of Bath, and d. 20 Jan. 1833.   (B.L.G. 1937 ed.)

6. All black background
Argent a lion rampant gules between three trefoils slipped vert (Livesay)
Crest: A lion's gamb erect gules   Mantling: Gules and argent
Frame decorated with skulls and crossbones
For General John Livesay, who d. 23 Feb. 1717.   (M.I.)

SHARNBROOK

1. Sinister background black
Ermine on a chief gules a label of three points or (Bullock), impaling, Vert a sword in bend argent hilted or between two ducal coronets or, on a chief argent three caltraps gules (Brownsword)
Motto: Mors janua vitæ   Cherub's head above
For Sarah, wife of John Bullock.   She d. 20 Apr. 1763, aged 34. (M.I.)

2. All black background
Arms: As 1.
Crest: A mural coronet argent through which are six arrows in saltire, three and three, points downwards argent feathered or   Mantling: Gules and argent   Motto: In coelo quies   Skull below
For John Bullock, d. 20 July 1764, aged 50.   (M.I.)

LITTLE STAUGHTON

1. All black background
Qly, 1st and 4th, Gules on two bars argent six mascles three and three gules, on a canton or a leopard's face azure (Gery), 2nd and 3rd, Azure on a saltire argent between four escallops or a battleaxe sable (Wade), impaling, Qly, 1st and 4th, Azure on a chevron argent three millrinds sable, on a canton or a trefoil slipped sable (Milnes), 2nd and 3rd, Gery
Crests: Dexter, An antelope's head argent armed or, the neck per saltire gules and argent charged with four mascles counterchanged
Sinister, On a mount vert a rhinoceros or charged with a battleaxe sable   No mantling   Motto: Resurgam
For William Hugh Wade-Gery, of Bushmead Priory, who m. 1829, Anne Beckingham (d. 11 Dec. 1852), dau. of John Milnes, of Beckingham, co. Lincoln, and d. 1 Sept. 1870.   (B.L.G. 1937 ed.; M.I.)

TEMPSFORD

1. Dexter background black
Per pale ermine and sable ermined argent, on a chevron counterchanged between three fleurs-de-lys or four lozenges counterchanged (Addington), impaling, Azure on a chevron the point ending in a cross formy or, between in chief two stags' heads erased or murally gorged gules and in base a lion rampant or, three fleurs-de-lys azure (   )
Crest: A leopard sejant guardant argent semy of roundels sable
Mantling: Gules and argent   Motto: Resurgam
Unidentified

Bedfordshire

(This hatchment, formerly in Tempsford church, is now in the possession of J. P. Addington, Colesden, Bedford)

THURLEIGH

1. **Dexter background black**
Gules on a bend argent three trefoils slipped vert (Harvey), impaling, Or a lion rampant within a double tressure flory counterflory sable, a molet sable for difference (Buchanan)
Crest: A leopard's head erased proper ducally gorged or
Mantling: Gules and argent   Motto: Ne oubliray iamais
For John Harvey, who m. 1677, Sarah, dau. of John Buchanan, of St Dunstan's-in-the-West, and d. 14 July 1715.   (Foster's Marriage Licences; Beds. Record Office)

TINGRITH

1. **All black background**
Per bend sinister ermine and sable ermined argent a lion rampant or (Trevor), impaling, Argent on a chevron azure between three trefoils slipped sable three crescents or (Williamson)
Crest: On a chapeau gules and ermine a wyvern sable
Mantling: Gules and argent   Motto: Resurgam
For Robert Trevor, of Tingrith House, who m. 1795, Mary Williamson, and d. 16 Feb. 1834. She d. 5 Jan. 1830.   (B.L.G. 1937 ed.)

TODDINGTON

1. **Sinister background black**
Gules on a chevron between three lions passant guardant argent each holding a battleaxe or in his dexter paw three lozenges sable, on a chief engrailed or a lozenge gules between two martlets sable (Cooper)
In pretence: Qly gules and azure, on a chevron ermine between three lions passant guardant or three mascles gules (Cooper)
For Elizabeth, dau. and heiress of John Cooper, of Toddington, who m. William Dodge Cooper Cooper (who dropped his paternal name of Heap and assumed the name and arms of Cooper in 1819), and d. 6 June 1855, aged 72.   (B.L.G. 5th ed.; M.I.)

2. **All black background**
Arms: As 1.   Crest: A lion sejant or holding in its dexter paw a battleaxe proper   Mantling: Gules and argent   Motto: Tuum est
For William Dodge Cooper Cooper, who d. 9 Aug. 1860, aged 77.
(Sources, as 1).

OLD WARDEN

1. Dexter background black
Qly, 1st and 4th, Argent a fess gules (Ongley), 2nd and 3rd, Argent three piles issuing from the chief gules, in base a mount vert, on a canton azure a sun in splendour or (Ongley)　In pretence: Argent a bend gules between three choughs proper, on a chief azure three horses' heads couped argent (Gosfright)
Baron's coronet　Crest: Arising from flames a phoenix proper
Motto: Mihi cura futuri　Supporters: Two griffins argent collared gules chained sable　All on a mantle gules and ermine
For Robert, 1st Baron Ongley, né Henley, who assumed the name and arms of Ongley on succeeding to the estates of Sir Samuel Ongley, and cr. Baron Ongley in 1776. He m. 1763, Frances, dau. and co-heir of Richard Gosfright, of Langton Hall, Essex, and d. 23 Oct. 1785.

2. All black background
On a lozenge surmounted by a baroness's coronet
Qly, 1st and 4th, Argent a fess gules (Ongley), 2nd and 3rd, Argent a chief indented gules, in base a mount vert, on a canton azure a sun in splendour or (Ongley)　In pretence: Gosfright
Supporters and mantle: As 1.
For Frances, widow of Robert, 1st Baron Ongley. She d. 22 Jan. 1799.
(Complete Peerage)

3. Dexter background black
Ongley, as 2nd and 3rd of 1., impaling, Gules a chevron or between three talbots passant argent, on a chief embattled argent three martlets azure (Burgoyne)
Baron's coronet　Crest: A phoenix rising or in its beak a bomb fired proper　Motto, supporters and mantle: As 1.
For Robert, 2nd Baron Ongley, who m. 1801, Frances, only dau. of Lt.-Gen. Sir John Burgoyne, 7th Bt., and d. 20 Aug. 1814.
(B.P. 1875 ed.)

4. All black background
On a lozenge surmounted by a baroness's coronet
Qly, as 2., but chief dancetty, impaling, Qly, 1st and 4th, Burgoyne, 2nd and 3rd, qly i. & iv. Argent three fusils conjoined in fess gules a bordure sable (Montagu), ii. & iii. Or an eagle displayed vert (Monthermer)　Supporters: As 1., but chained or
For Frances, widow of Robert, 2nd Baron Ongley, d. 27 Dec. 1841.
(B.P. 1875 ed.; M.I.)

5. All black background
Sable on a chevron between six crosses formy fitchy argent three fleurs-de-lys azure (Smith)

Bedfordshire

Knight's helm   Crest: A heron's head erased proper in its beak a fish proper   Mantling: Gules and argent   Motto: In coelo quies
For Sir William Smyth, who d. 8 Sept. 1741, aged 79.   (M.I.)

WESTONING

1. Dexter background black
Azure three annulets between two bars and three crosses formy or (for Coventry-Campion), impaling, Argent on a fess between three cross crosslets fitchy sable a cinquefoil argent (Lawton)
Crest: A goat's head erased ermine entwined with a snake proper
Mantling: Azure and or   Motto: Aien apisteyein
For the Rev. John William Coventry-Campion, son of John Coventry and Biddy Campion, Lord of the Manor of Westoning, who m. Ann, and d. 23 June 1893, aged 79.   (M.I. in churchyard)

WOBURN Abbey

1. Sinister background black
Argent a lion rampant gules, on a chief sable three escallops argent (Russell), impaling, Argent on a cross gules five escallops or (Villiers)
Motto: Che sara sara   Supporters: Dexter, A lion gules
Sinister, A heraldic antelope gules   Cherub's head above
For Charlotte Anne, eldest dau. of George, 4th Earl of Jersey, who m. Lord William Russell, grandson of John, 4th Duke of Bedford, K.G., and d. 31 Aug. 1808.   (B.P. 1949 ed.)
(There is another hatchment for Lady Charlotte Russell in the parish church at Chenies, Bucks)

WOOTTON

1. Dexter background black
Argent on a chevron sable between three oak leaves proper three bezants, in centre chief the Badge of Ulster (Monoux), impaling, Azure an eagle displayed argent (Cotton)
Crest: A dove azure winged or, in its beak a sprig of oakleaves proper fructed or   Mantling: Gules and argent
For Sir Humphrey Monoux, 2nd Bt., who m. Alice, dau. of Sir Thomas Cotton, Bt. of Conington, Hunts, and d. 31 July 1685, aged 44.
(B.E.B.; M.I.)

2. Dexter background black
Monoux, as 1., impaling, Or on a chief indented sable three crescents argent (Harvey)

Crest and mantling: As 1.   Motto: Mors iter ad vitam   Frame decorated with winged skulls, crossbones and hourglasses
For Sir Philip Monoux, 3rd Bt., who m. Dorothy, eldest dau. of William Harvey, of Chigwell, and d. 25 Nov. 1707, aged 28.   (B.E.B.; M.I.)

3. All black background
On a lozenge   Arms: As 2., but Badge of Ulster over impalement line
For Dorothy, widow of Sir Philip Monoux, 3rd Bt., d. 22 May 1758, aged 74.   (B.E.B.; M.I.)

4. Sinister background black
Argent on a chevron sable between three oakleaves proper three bezants, on a chief gules a dove between two anchors erect argent, a crescent sable for difference (Monoux), impaling, Sable on a chevron or between three cinquefoils ermine five gouttes gules (Wodehouse)
Motto: Mors iter ad vitam
For Lucy, dau. of Edmund Wodehouse, who m. Lewis Monoux, and d. 3 Feb. 1704. He d. 30 Mar. 1720, aged 70.   (B.E.B.; M.I.)

5. Sinister background black
Argent on a chevron sable between three maple leaves proper three bezants (Monoux), impaling, Argent six lions rampant three, two and one sable (Savage)
Motto: In coelo quies
For Mary, dau. of Thomas Savage, who m. as his 1st wife, Humphrey Monoux, and d. 22 Mar. 1741, aged 38.   (M.I.; B.E.B.)

6. Sinister background black
Monoux, as 5., impaling, Gules a lion passant per pale or and argent between in chief two and in base two cross crosslets argent (Astell)
Motto: In coelo quies   Cherub's head above and skull below
For Elizabeth, dau. of William Astell, who m. as his 2nd wife, Humphrey Monoux, and d. 19 May 1747, aged 44.   (M.I.)

7. Dexter background black
Argent on a chevron sable between three oak leaves proper three bezants (Monoux), impaling, Sable a fess between three fleurs-de-lys argent (Welby)   Crest and mantling: As 1.   Motto: Mors janua vitæ
Frame decorated with skulls and crossbones
For Humphrey Monoux, who m. 3rd, Selina, dau. of Richard Welby, and d. 18 May 1752, aged 50.   (M.I.)

8. Dexter background black
Monoux, as 7., in centre chief the Badge of Ulster   In pretence: Qly, 1st and 4th, Azure three salmon naiant fesswise in pale argent (Sambrook), 2nd and 3rd, Or on a bend gules three cinquefoils argent

Bedfordshire 21

(Vanaker)   Crest: As 1., but fructed or   Mantling: Gules and argent
Motto: As 7
For Sir Humphrey Monoux, 4th Bt., who m. Elizabeth, dau. of Sir
Samuel Sambrook, and d. 3 Dec. 1757, aged 55.   (M.I.)

9. All black background
On a lozenge surmounted by a cherub's head   Arms: As 8.
Motto: In coelo quies   Skull below
For Elizabeth, widow of Sir Humphrey Monoux, 4th Bt., d. 4 Sept.
1770, aged 65.   (M.I.)

10. All black background
On a lozenge surmounted by a cherub's head
Monoux, as 7., in chief the Badge of Ulster, impaling, Argent a saltire
and in base an eagle displayed sable (Riddell)
For Elizabeth, dau. of Ambrose Riddell, who m. Sir Philip Monoux,
5th Bt., and d. 13 Aug. 1814, aged 75. He d. 17 Apr. 1805, aged 66.
(B.E.B.; M.I.)

11. All black background
Monoux, as 7., in chief the Badge of Ulster
Crest: A dove proper in its beak an oak leaf proper   Mantling: Gules
and argent   Motto: In coelo quies   Winged skull below
For Sir Philip Monoux, 6th Bt., who d. unm. 27 Feb. 1809, aged 38.
(B.E.B.; M.I.)

12. Dexter background black
Monoux, as 7., with Badge of Ulster over impalement line, impaling,
Argent on a bend gules cotised and between two garbs sable three pairs
of wings conjoined in lure points downwards argent (Wingfield)
Crest: A dove azure in its beak an oak leaf proper   Mantling and
motto: As 11.   Skull below
For the Rev. Sir Philip Monoux, 7th and last Bt., who d.s.p. 3 Feb.
1814.   (B.E.B.)

13. All black background
On a lozenge suspended from blue ribbons
Qly, 1st and 4th, Gules a fess between two lions passant argent (Payne),
2nd and 3rd, Monoux, as 7.
For Augusta, b. 1801, only dau. of Sir John Payne and Mary Monoux.
She d. unm. 4 Dec. 1852.   (Ped. in Beds. Record Office; MS Ped. Soc.
of Gen.)

BERKSHIRE

by

Peter Summers

Avington: For William James, 1666
(*Photograph by Mr. J. E. Titterton*)

INTRODUCTION

Only fifty-five hatchments have been recorded in the county, but they are not lacking in interest. The earliest is at Avington, for William James who died in 1666. It is typical of the period, being small, on a wood panel, and with the frame decorated with emblems of mortality. There are five of the present century, three being at Bessels Leigh; but the latest is at Pusey, for Sir Philip Francis Bouverie-Pusey, who died in 1933. The largest number in one church may be seen at Pangbourne, all of the Breedon family, who lived at Bere Court in the parish. These have presented problems in identification as no printed pedigrees exist, and no members of the family have been traced.

The hatchment of Sir George Bowyer at Radley has one very unusual feature; his arms bear two Badges of Ulster. Sir George held two baronetcies, being the 6th baronet of Denham, and the 2nd of Radley.

At Ufton Nervet are the hatchments of William and Mary Thoyts. The Thoyts arms and crest are both charged with the sign of the planet Venus, and Mary's coat (she was formerly a Newman), bears as an Augmentation of Honour an escutcheon sable charged with a crowned portcullis or. This was granted to her ancestor, Colonel Newman, for his distinguished conduct at the battle of Worcester. Another unusual crest, reminiscent of that of Stanley, may be seen on a Venables hatchment at Cookham; it depicts a child in a fish weir being preyed upon by a wyvern, which is itself transfixed through the neck by an arrow. A strange device, indeed, but one for which there must surely be some explanation.

At Buckland there are four Throckmorton hatchments, three in the parish church, and one in the R.C. church close by, for Robert Throckmorton, who presumably turned to Rome, and died in 1853. It is a very small example, not more than 18 ins. x 18 ins., and so was not likely to have been hung in the customary manner over the front door during the period of mourning. The hatchment in the parish church of Mary, 1st wife of Charles Throckmorton (later to succeed as 7th baronet), is remarkable in that the Throckmorton arms do not appear at all! Their place is taken by the arms of Courtenay. Charles' father assumed the additional name and arms of Courtenay on succeeding to the Molland estate.

Peter Summers

ALDERMASTON

1. All black background
Sable a chevron between three battleaxes argent (Congreve)   In pretence: Qly, 1st, Gules a cross lozengy argent (Stawell), 2nd, Sable a chevron engrailed between three arrows points downwards argent (Forster), 3rd, Gules two lions passant guardant argent (Delamere), 4th, Or a bend fusilly sable (Archard)
Crest: A falcon rising proper   Mantling: Gules and argent   Motto: In coelo quies   Skull in base
For Ralph Congreve, who m. Charlotte, dau. and heir of William, Lord Stawell, by Elizabeth, dau. of Sir Humphrey Forster, and d. 6 Dec. 1775, aged 57.   (M.I.)

2. Dexter background black
Congreve, impaling, to dexter, Argent six lions rampant sable langued gules (Savage), and to sinister, Argent a lion rampant sable (Jones)
Crest: As 1.   Motto: Spes mea in Deo   Cherub's head below shield and palm branches at sides
For the Rev. Richard Congreve, who m. 1st, Elizabeth, dau. of Thomas Savage, of Elmley Castle, and 2nd, Martha, dau. and heiress of John Jones, of Fynnant, Mont., and d. 27 July 1782.   (B.L.G. 5th ed.; Berry's Berkshire Genealogies)

3. All black background
On a lozenge surmounted by a cherub's head
Congreve, impaling, Jones
Skull in base
For Martha, widow of the Rev. Richard Congreve. She d. 19 Mar. 1809. (Sources, as 2.)

4. Sinister background black
Congreve   In pretence: Argent a chevron gules between three pinecones vert, on a canton azure a fleur-de-lys or (Peperell)
Motto: In coelo quies   Cherub's head above
For Mary, 2nd dau. of Sir William Peperell, of Boston, Mass., who m. 1799, William Congreve, eldest son of the Rev. Richard Congreve, and d. 3 Feb. 1839.   (B.L.G. 5th ed.; Berks. Arch. Journal, XLII, pt. 1)

5. All black background
Arms: As 4.
Crest: A falcon rising proper belled or   Mantling and motto: As 1.
For William Congreve, who d. 17 Mar. 1843. (Sources, as 4.)

APPLETON

1. All black background
Or a chevron between three apples gules a molet for difference
(Southby)   Crest: A demi-lion rampant or holding in his dexter paw
an apple gules   Mantling: Gules and argent   Motto: In Deo spes
mea
Probably for John, 3rd son of Robert Southby, d. 1733, aged 84.
(Berry's Berkshire Genealogies)
(This hatchment is no longer in the church; it was handed over by a
previous incumbent to a member of the Southby family)

ARDINGTON

1. Dexter background black
Qly of nine, 1st, Argent on a fess between three crosses formy sable
three roundels argent (Clarke), 2nd, Argent two lozenges conjoined in
fess gules in chief a martlet sable for difference (Champney), 3rd, Or on
a cross azure five mascles or (Pikeman), 4th, Sable a chevron ermine
between three cronels argent (Wiseman), 5th, Paly of six argent and
sable over all a fess gules (Blyant), 6th, Vert a lion rampant argent
armed and langued gules crowned or (Bresworth), 7th, Gules three
fusils conjoined in fess ermine between three martlets argent (Rokele),
8th, Or on a chevron between three cinquefoils azure three escallops
argent, on a chief gules a griffin passant argent (Hawkins), 9th, Gules
a fess vair between in chief a bezant charged with an anchor sable
between two molets of six points or and in base three martlets argent
(Bayley), impaling, Qly, 1st and 4th, Gules on a chevron or three
molets sable, in base a stag's head erased or, within a bordure or (Kerr),
2nd, Or a cross patonce sable over all a bendlet gules (Nelson), 3rd,
Barry of six gules and argent over all a bend vairy or and sable (Nelson)
Crest: A cross formy or between two wings argent   Mantling: Gules
and argent   Motto: Absit ut glorier nisi in cruce   Cherub's head
below
For William Wiseman Clarke, who m. 2nd, Elizabeth, dau. of John
Kerr, by Mary, sister and heir of Richard Walter Nelson, of
Chaddleworth, and d. 4 Sept. 1826.   (Burke's Commoners, I, 112;
P. S. Spokes)

AVINGTON

1. Dexter background black
Qly of six, 1st and 6th, Gules a dolphin embowed or (James), 2nd, Per
chief argent and or, over all a lion rampant gules langued azure
(Goodlake), 3rd, Ermine on a chief indented azure three griffins'

heads erased or (Caplen), 4th, Sable a falcon argent beaked and belled or (Bolton), 5th, Gules three wolves' heads erased or (   ), impaling, Qly, 1st and 4th, Or a chevron between three apples gules stalked vert (Southby), 2nd and 3rd, Sable a chevron ermine between three cronels argent (Wiseman)
Crests: Dexter, An ostrich proper   Sinister, A demi-lion rampant gules holding in the dexter paw an apple gules stalked vert
Mantling: Gules and argent   Motto: J'aime a jamais
On a wood panel in frame decorated with skulls, crossbones and hourglasses   A small hatchment, c. 2½ ft x 2½ ft
For William James, who m. Sarah, dau. of John Southby, of Carswell, and d. 1666. She d. 21 Dec. 1699, aged 75.   (M.I.)

BARKHAM

1. All black background
On a lozenge surmounted by a cherub's head
Qly, 1st and 4th, Barry of eight argent and gules a cross flory sable (Gower), 2nd and 3rd, Azure three laurel leaves or (Leveson), impaling, Argent a cross engrailed per pale gules and sable (Broke)
Motto: Resurgemus
For Isabella Mary, dau. of Philip Bowes Broke, of Broke Hall, Suffolk, who m. 1796, General John Leveson-Gower, and d. 28 May 1817. (B.P. 1949 ed.)

BESSELS LEIGH

1. All black background
Sable a bend fusilly argent, a crescent for difference (Lenthall)
Crest: A greyhound courant sable   Mantling: Azure, gules and argent
Motto: Spes mea in Deo   A small hatchment, c. 2½ ft x 2½ ft
Possibly for Philip John Lenthall, d. unm. 1864.   (B.L.G. 1937 ed.)

2. All black background
Lenthall arms only, no crescent
Crest: The Heneage knot reversed   Mantling: Gules and azure, ending in tassels
Possibly for Edmund Kyffin Lenthall, who d. unm. 24 July 1907. (B.L.G. 1937 ed.)

3. All black background
Lenthall, as 2., impaling, Azure in chief two lions rampant combatant argent upholding a dexter hand couped apaumy proper, all between three pierced molets gules, in base a salmon naiant in water proper (Donnelly)

Crest: A greyhound courant sable collared or   Mantling: Gules, azure
and argent   Motto: Spes mea in Deo
For Walter Ellison Lenthall, who m. 1859, Frances Mary, dau. of
Michael Ross Donnelly, and d. 4 June 1908.   (B.L.G. 1937 ed.)

4. All black background
Lenthall, with a pierced molet for difference
Crest, mantling and motto: As 3.   Pierced molet below shield
Possibly for Edmund Henry Lenthall, who d. 18 May 1909.   (B.L.G. 1937 ed.)

BLEWBURY

1. All black background
Azure a cross countercompony or and gules between four roundels argent (Crutchfield), impaling, Argent a chevron sable, on a chief sable three martlets argent (Wilde)
No crest   Mantling: Gules and argent   Motto: In coelo quies
Cherubs' heads at top corners of shield, and skull in base
For William Crutchfield, who m. 1748, Mary Wilde, and d. 6 Sept. 1775. (Church guide; par. regs.)

BUCKLAND

1. Dexter background black
Qly, 1st and 4th, Gules on a chevron argent three bars gemel sable (Throckmorton), 2nd and 3rd, Argent a fess between three gates sable (Yate), over all the Badge of Ulster, impaling, Argent three roundels between two bendlets and a bordure gules (Heywood)
Crest: An elephant's head sable tusked and eared or   Mantling: Gules and argent   Motto; Virtus sola nobilitas
For Sir Robert Throckmorton, 4th Bt., who m. 3rd, 1763, Lucy, dau. of James Heywood, of Marlstow, Devon, and d. 8 Dec. 1791.
(B.P. 1949 ed)

2. Dexter background black
Qly, as 1., with Badge of Ulster, impaling, Azure three stirrups leathered or (Giffard)
Crest: As 1., but tusked argent   Mantling and motto: As 1.
For Sir John Courtenay Throckmorton, 5th Bt., who m. 1782, Maria Catherine, dau. of Thomas Giffard, of Chillington, and d.s.p. 3 Jan. 1819. (Source, as 1.)
(There is another hatchment for Sir John at Coughton, Warwickshire)

Berkshire

3. Sinister background black
On three roundels gules a crescent sable for difference (Courtenay), impaling, Azure a fess dancetty the two upper points fleurs-de-lys or (Plowden)   Motto: In coelo quies   Two cherubs' heads above, and elaborate gold scroll work at sides
For Mary, dau. of Edmund Plowden, of Plowden, Salop, who m. 1787, Charles Throckmorton (succeeded as 7th Bt. 1826), and d. 24 May 1825, aged 60. Sir George Throckmorton, 6th Bt. assumed the additional name and arms of Courtenay on inheriting the estates at Molland in Devon.   (B.P. 1949 ed.)   Charles evidently went one step further and assumed the Courtenay arms only, though the Throckmorton arms appear on his hatchment at Coughton, Warwickshire.

BUCKLAND R.C.Church

1. All black background
Throckmorton, with label of three points argent
Crest: An elephant's head sable tusked and eared or   Mantling: Gules and argent
A very small hatchment, c. 1½ ft x 1½ ft, inscribed on frame, Robt Chas C. Throckmorton, Died 14th December 1853.

BUCKLEBURY

1. All black background
Gules a chevron between three crosses flory or, in centre chief the Badge of Ulster (Rich)
Crest: A wyvern argent   Mantling: Gules and argent   Motto: Resurgam
For Sir George Rich, 6th Bt., who d. unm. 8 Jan. 1799.   (B.E.B.; M.I.)

2. Dexter background black
Qly of nine, 1st and 9th, Argent on a cross quarterpierced azure between two martlets in dexter chief and sinister base sable four cinquefoils or (Hartley), 2nd, Gules a cross lozengy or between four roses argent (Packer), 3rd, Per chevron sable and argent in chief two eagles displayed or (Stephens), 4th, Azure on a chevron engrailed between three eagles displayed or three fleurs-de-lys azure, on a chief or a fleur-delys between two ermine spots azure (Winchcombe), 5th, Gules on a bend between six cross crosslets fitchy argent the Augmentation of Flodden (Howard), 6th, Gules three lions passant guardant in pale or a label of three points argent (Brotherton), 7th, Chequy or and azure (Warren), 8th, Gules a lion rampant argent (Mowbray), impaling, Argent a

greyhound courant sable, on a chief indented sable three bezants
(Blackwell)
Crest: A martlet sable holding in its beak a cross crosslet fitchy or
Mantling: Gules and argent   Motto: Resurgam
For Winchcombe Henry Hartley, who m. 1st, Mary (d. 15 Apr. 1786),
eldest dau. of Samuel Blackwell, of Williamstrip Park, co. Gloucs, and
2nd, Anne Blackwell, her sister, and d. 12 Aug. 1794, aged 54.
(B.L.G. 7th ed.; M.I.)

3. All black background
On a lozenge surmounted by a cherub's head
Qly of nine, 1st and 9th, Hartley, 2nd, Gules a cross lozengy between
four roses argent (Packer), 3rd, Stephens, 4th, Azure on a chevron
engrailed between three eagles close or three cinquefoils azure, on a
chief or a fleur-de-lys between two spearheads azure (Winchcombe),
5th, Howard, 6th, Brotherton, 7th, Warren, 8th, Mowbray, impaling,
Argent a greyhound courant sable collared gules, on a chief indented
sable three bezants (Blackwell)
For Anne, widow of Winchcombe Henry Hartley. She d.
(B.L.G. 7th ed.; M.I.)

4. Dexter background black
Qly of nine, 1st and 9th, Hartley, 2nd, Packer as 3., 3rd, Stephens,
4th, Winchcombe as 3., but fleur-de-lys and spearheads sable, 5th,
Howard, 6th, Brotherton, 7th, Warren, 8th, Mowbray, impaling, Azure
three arrows palewise in fess points downwards or barbed and flighted
argent, on a chief or three Moors' heads couped in profile sable (Watts)
Crest, mantling and motto: As 2.
For the Rev. Winchcombe Henry Howard Hartley, who m. 1809,
Elizabeth, eldest dau. of Thomas Watts, of Bath, and d. 9 Sept. 1832,
aged 44. (B.L.G. 7th ed.; M.I.)

5. All black background
On a curvilinear lozenge surmounted by a cherub's head
Qly of nine, 1st and 9th, Hartley, 2nd, Packer as 2., 3rd, Per chevron
sable and argent in chief two eagles displayed argent (Stephens), 4th,
Winchcombe as 3. but cinquefoils sable, 5th, Howard, 6th, Brotherton,
7th, Warren, 8th, Mowbray, impaling, Watts
Motto: Resurgam
For Elizabeth, widow of the Rev. Winchcombe Henry Howard Hartley.
She d. 17 May 1840, aged 50.   (B.L.G. 7th ed.; M.I.)

6. All black background
Paly of six argent and azure, on a bend gules a molet in chief argent
(Annesley), impaling, Gules three bars ermine (   )
Crest: A Moor's head couped in profile proper, wreathed at the temples
argent and azure and wearing earrings argent

Mantling: Gules and argent   Motto: In coelo quies
Probably for the Rev. Martin Annesley, D.D., Vicar of Bucklebury, who m. 2nd, 1732, Mary, 3rd dau. and co-heir of William Hanbury, of Much Marcle, and d. June 1749. The name of his 1st wife is not known. (B.L.G. 2nd ed.; B.P. 1949 ed., Valentia)
(All six hatchments have been recently restored by Lt.-Col. R. L. V. ffrench Blake)

COOKHAM

1. All black background
On a lozenge surmounted by a cherub's head
Qly, 1st and 4th, Argent an oak tree eradicated proper surmounted by a fess azure charged with three molets or (Watson), 2nd and 3rd, Azure three dexter hands apaumy couped at the wrist and erect proper (   )
In pretence: Azure a fess argent fretty sable between three greyhounds sejant argent collared sable (Gale)   Motto: In coelo quies   Skull below
For Penelope Gale, of North Town, who m. William Watson, of Queen Square, Bloomsbury, and d. 19 Oct. 1848, aged 90.   (M.I.; Annual Register, 1848)

2. All black background
On a lozenge surmounted by a cherub's head
Chequy argent and gules a lion rampant guardant or (Pocock), impaling, Argent on a bend cotised sable three lions rampant argent (Browne)
Mantling: Gules and argent   Motto: Resurgam
For Anne, widow of Peter Joye, of Biggin, Northants, who m. Sir Isaac Pocock, of Maidenhead, and d. 6 July 1818. He d. 8 Oct. 1810.
(College of Arms)

3. All black background
On a lozenge surmounted by a cherub's head
Chequy ermine and gules a lion rampant guardant or (Pocock), impaling, Per pale azure and gules three lions rampant argent (Evans)
Motto: Resurgam
For Anne Evans, who m. Nicholas Pocock, and d. 27 Dec. 1827. He d. 9 Mar. 1821.   (Source, as 2.)

4. Dexter background black
Azure two bars argent (Venables), impaling, Ermine a chevron between three fleurs-de-lys or (Fromond)
Crest: A child in a fish weir proper preyed on by a wyvern gules transfixed through the neck with an arrow argent   Mantling: Gules and argent   Motto: Nous persevons

For William Venables, F.S.A., Lord Mayor of London, 1825-6, who m. Ann Ruth Fromow, and d. 31 July 1840. (D.N.B.)

5. Dexter background black
Vert a cross patonce or (?Brant), impaling, Or on a fess dancetty azure between three lions rampant gules three roundels argent (Rowles) Crest: An elephant caparisoned proper   Mantling: Gules and argent   Motto: Resurgam
Probably for James Brant, of Ditton House, Cookham, who m. Elizabeth Rowles, and was bur. 29 May 1819, aged 62. (P.R.O.)

6. All black background
On a lozenge surmounted by a cherub's head
Arms: As 5.
Motto: In coelo quies   Skull below
Probably for Elizabeth, widow of James Brant, bur. 14 May 1832, aged 72. (P.R.O.)

FARINGDON

1. Dexter background black
Ermine a bend lozengy gules (Pye), impaling, Ermine a fess chequy or and azure between three talbots passant sable (Warren) Crest: A cross crosslet fitchy gules between two wings conjoined at the base displayed argent   Mantling: Gules and argent   Motto: In cruce glorior
For Henry Pye, who m. 1732, as his third wife, Isabella Warren, and d. 6 Jan. 1749, aged 65.   (M.I.)

KINGSTON LISLE

1. Dexter background black
Qly, 1st and 4th, Argent on a cross cotised flory sable between four molets pierced azure five martlets or (Atkins), 2nd and 3rd, Or a tree on a mount proper between two crescents in fess gules (Martin), impaling, Ermine five barrulets gules over all three escutcheons or (Halhed)
Crests: Dexter, A Bengal tiger statant or, over it the motto, Libertas   Sinister, Two greyhounds' heads addorsed and erased, the dexter argent the sinister sable, gorged with an antique crown counterchanged, over it the motto, Quaere superna   Motto (below): Cuncta mundana rotantur   All on a mantle gules and ermine
For Edwin Martin, who took the additional name of Atkins, on succeeding to the manor of Kingston Lisle. He m. Ellen Frances (d. 1831), dau. of William Halhed, and d. 30 July 1799. (B.L.G. 5th ed.)

Berkshire 35

2. All black background
Qly, 1st and 4th, Martin, 2nd and 3rd, Argent on a cross cotised flory sable between four molets gules each charged with another or five martlets or (Atkins), impaling, Chequy or and ermine a lion rampant gules, on a chief sable a leopard's face between two swords points downwards or (Cook)
Crests: As 1., but no mottoes above   Mantling: Gules and argent
Motto: In coelo quies
For Atkins Edwin Martin-Atkins, son of Edwin Martin-Atkins. He m. Ann, younger dau. of John Cook of Hothorpe, and d. 1 May 1825, aged 46.   (B.L.G. 5th ed.; Annual Register)

MILTON Manor

1. Sinister background black
Gules on a chief indented argent three escallops gules (Barrett), impaling, Sable a chevron engrailed between three greyhounds' heads erased ermine (Belson)
Motto: In te Domine speravi   Cherubs' heads
For Mary, dau. of John Belson, who m. as his 1st wife, Bryant Barrett, of Milton Manor, and d. 9 Dec. 1768.   (per Mrs. Mockler)

PANGBOURNE

1. Dexter background black
Gules a lion rampant argent between eight nails or (Breedon), impaling, Gules a fess between eight billets or (May)
Crest: A demi-lion rampant holding in its dexter paw a cross formy fitchy gules   Mantling: Gules and argent   Motto: Resurgam
For the Rev. John Symonds Breedon, D.D., F.S.A., of Bere Court, Rector of Pangbourne, son of Henry Symonds, assumed name and arms of Breedon on succeeding to estates, m. Jane, dau. and co-heir of Daniel May, of Pangbourne, and d. 3 Aug. 1826, aged 72.
(M.I.; MS Ped., Soc. of Gen.)

2. All black background
On a lozenge surmounted by a cherub's head
Arms: As 1.
Motto: In coelo quies
For Jane, widow of the Rev. John Symonds Breedon, d. 19 Apr. 1836, aged 69.   (Sources, as 1.)

3. Dexter background black
Breedon, impaling, Vert a saltire engrailed argent (Hawley)
Crest, mantling and motto: As 1.

For John Symonds Breedon, eldest son of John Symonds Breedon and Jane May, who m. Catherine Toovey, dau. of Lt.-Col. Henry William Toovey Hawley, of West Green House, Hants, and d. 5 May 1843. (MS ped.; B.L.G. 5th ed.; M.I.)

4. All black background
Breedon arms only   To dexter of main shield, Breedon, impaling, Or a bend engrailed vert plain cotised sable (Hanbury) S.Bl.   To sinister of main shield, Breedon, impaling, Or a lion rampant reguardant sable (Pryse) D.Bl.
Crest and mantling: As 1.   Motto: In coelo quies   Skull in base
For John Breedon, who m. 1st, Mary Hanbury, and 2nd, Elizabeth Pryse, of Hammersmith, and d. 14 Nov. 1776.   (M.I.; Letter, Berks Rec. Office; Harl. MS.)

5. Dexter background black
Breedon, impaling, Argent two bars and in chief three molets sable (Allen)   Crest, mantling and motto: As 1.
For Charles Breedon, who m. Louisa Allen, and d. 20 Aug. 1844. (M.I.)

6. Dexter background black
Breedon, impaling, Per bend sinister rompu argent and sable six martlets counterchanged (Alleyn)
Crowned winged skull on helm in place of crest   Mantling: Gules and argent   Motto: In coelo quies
Possibly for John Breedon, b. 1742, d. 16 Jan. 1783. (M.I.)

7. All black background
Breedon arms only, with label of three points argent for difference
Crest, mantling and motto: As 1.
For John, eldest son of John Symonds Breedon and Catherine Toovey Hawley, who d. 27 May 1843, aged 23. (M.I.)

PUSEY

1. All black background
Qly, 1st and 4th, Gules three bars argent (Pusey), 2nd and 3rd, Per fess or and argent a double-headed eagle displayed sable langued gules, on the breast an escutcheon gules charged with a bend vair (Bouverie), impaling, Argent a chevron between three roundels gules (Sherard)
Crest: A cat passant guardant tail extended argent   Mantling: Gules and argent   Motto: Resurgam
For the Hon. Philip Bouverie-Pusey, who m. 1798, Lucy, eldest dau. of Robert, 4th Earl of Harborough, and d. 14 Apr. 1828. She d. 27 Mar. 1858. (B.L.G. 1937 ed.)

Berkshire

2. Sinister background black
Qly, as 1., impaling, Qly, 1st and 4th, Per pale azure and gules three
lions rampant argent langued gules (Herbert), 2nd and 3rd, Chequy
argent and sable a fess gules (Acland)
Mantling: Gules and argent   Motto: Resurgam   Cherub's head
above
For Emily Frances Theresa, 2nd dau. of Henry George, 2nd Earl of
Carnarvon, who m. 1822, Philip Pusey, and d. 16 Nov. 1854.
(B.L.G. 1937 ed.)

3. All black background
Arms: As 2.
Crests: Dexter, as 1.   Sinister, A demi-doubleheaded eagle sable
ducally gorged or and charged on the breast with a cross flory argent
Mantling and motto: As 1.
For Philip Pusey, d. 9 July 1855.   (B.L.G. 1937 ed.)

4. All black background
Sable a cross flory between four escallops argent on the cross a crescent
sable for difference (Fletcher), impaling, Qly, 1st and 4th, Pusey,
2nd and 3rd, Bouverie
Crest: A demi-lion rampant azure, armed argent langued gules ducally
gorged or   Mantling: Sable and argent   Motto: Resurgam
For Capt. Francis Charteris Fletcher, who m. 1862, Clara, dau. of
Philip Pusey, and d. 24 Jan. 1891. She d. 3 Feb. 1911.
(B.L.G. 1937 ed.)

5. Dexter background black
Qly, 1st and 4th, qly i. & iv. Gules three bars argent, on a canton
ermine a bugle horn stringed or (Pusey), ii. & iii. Bouverie, 2nd and 3rd,
Fletcher, impaling, Qly argent and sable on a bend gules three molets
argent (Cayley)
Crests: Dexter, A demi-doubleheaded eagle proper ducally gorged or
charged on the breast with a cross flory argent   Centre, A cat statant
guardant proper around its neck a bugle horn stringed or   Sinister,
A demi-bloodhound rampant azure langued gules ducally gorged or
Mantling: Gules and argent   Motto: Patria cara carior libertas
For Philip Francis Bouverie-Pusey, son of Capt. Francis Charteris
Fletcher by his wife Clara, dau. of Philip Pusey, m. 1916, Lucy Violet,
7th dau. of Digby Cayley, and d.s.p. 6 June 1933.   (B.L.G. 1937 ed.)

RADLEY

1. All black background
Qly of six, 1st, Or a bend vair cotised gules, in dexter and centre chief
the Badge of Ulster (Bowyer), 2nd, Azure three spades argent bladed or

(Knipersley), 3rd, Azure a bend or a bordure argent (Grosvenor), 4th, Azure two bars argent (Venables), 5th, Argent on a fess sable between three hawks volant azure a leopard's face or between two molets argent (Stonehouse), 6th, Argent crusilly a lion rampant azure (Brett), impaling, Argent a human heart gules imperially crowned or, on a chief azure three molets argent (Douglas)
Crests: Dexter, On a ducal coronet or a lion sejant argent   Centre, A falcon rising wings expanded sable belled or   Sinister, A demi-man shooting with a bow and arrow proper   Mantling: Gules and argent
Motto: Requiem æternam   All on a red and gold mantle with gold tassels
For Sir George Bowyer, 6th and 2nd Bt., who m. 1808, Anne Hammond, dau. of Capt. Sir Andrew Snape Douglas, R.N., and d. 1 July 1860.   (B.P. 1949 ed.)

SHINFIELD

1. Dexter background black
Gules on a chevron or three lions rampant sable (Cobham), impaling, Argent three horses' heads erased sable a chief gules (Slade)
Crest: A man's head in profile bearded proper, wearing a cap gules turned up or and sable buttoned at the top or   Mantling: Gules and argent   Motto: In coelo quies   Winged skull in base
For Alexander Cobham, who m. Charlotte (Slade), and d. 12 July 1809. She d. 5 Dec. 1830, aged 75.   (M.I.)

2. Sinister background black
Or three bars azure on a canton argent a chaplet gules (Hulme), impaling, Gules a lion rampant argent within an orle of eight nails or (Breedon)   Motto: Resurgam   Cherubs' heads at top angles of shield
For Elizabeth, dau. of the Rev. J. S. Breedon, D.D., of Bere Court, who m. the Rev. George Hulme, of Shinfield Green, and d. 2 Sept. 1827, aged 39.   (M.I.)

3. All black background
Barry of eight or and sable on a canton argent a chaplet gules (Hulme), impaling, Breedon
Crest: A lion's head erased gules wearing a chapeau gules and ermine
Mantling: Gules and argent   Motto: Resurgam
For the Rev. George Hulme, who d. 9 Feb. 1845.   (M.I.)

UFTON NERVET

1. Dexter background black
Azure on a fess between three molets of six points or two signs of the planet Venus sable (Thoyts)   In pretence: Qly sable and argent in the

Berkshire 39

first and fourth quarters three molets argent, an augmentation of an inescutcheon gules charged with a crowned portcullis or (Newman)
Crest: A heathcock rising proper charged with the sign of Venus or
Mantling: Gules and argent Motto: Resurgam
For William Thoyts, of Sulhamstead, who m. Jane, dau. and co-heir of Abram Newman of Mount Bures, Essex, and d. 26 Nov. 1817, aged 50. (B.L.G. 5th ed.; M.I.)

2. All black background
On a lozenge surmounted by a cherub's head
Arms: As 1.
For Jane, widow of William Thoyts. She d. 30 Oct. 1850, aged 88. (Sources, as 1.)
(Both these hatchments were originally in the church at Sulhamstead Bannister, which was demolished in 1967)

WINTERBOURNE

1. All black background
On a lozenge surmounted by a cherub's head
Or a chevron between three apples gules (Southby), impaling, Argent on a saltire sable five fleurs-de-lys or (Hawkins)
Motto: Spes mea in Deo
For Mary, dau. of John Hawkins, of Newbury, who m. 1803, Richard Southby, of Chieveley, and d. 1846, aged 71. He d. 24 Dec. 1824, aged 77. (B.L.G. 2nd ed.; M.I.)

2. Dexter background black
Argent three garbs within a double tressure flory counterflory gules (   ) In pretence, and impaling, Paly of six argent and gules three crescents sable (   )
Crest: A demi-lion argent holding a garb or banded gules Mantling: Gules and argent
Unidentified
(Notes on the History of Chieveley, by B. H. B. Attlee (1919), attributes this hatchment to Philip Henshaw, who m. Mabel, dau. and heiress of Sir Jemmett Raymond of Henwick, Thatcham, but the arms give no justification for this attribution)

LONG WITTENHAM

1. All black background
On a lozenge surmounted by a skull
Per bend sinister ermine and sable ermined argent a lion rampant or (Trevor), impaling, Azure a chevron between three griffins' heads

erased argent, on a chief or a lion passant between two roundels gules
(Jennens)
Motto: Mors janua vitæ
For Elizabeth, sister of William Jennens, who m. Tudor Trevor, and
d. 16 Mar. 1784, aged 86.   (M.I.)

BUCKINGHAMSHIRE

by

Peter Summers

Stoke Poges 10: For Granville Penn, 1844
(*Photograph by Mr. Tony Bunce*)

INTRODUCTION

There are few early hatchments in the county; that for Anthony Radcliffe at Chalfont St Giles, who died in 1718, is one of the earliest. But there is a very small, probably seventeenth century, hatchment at Stoke Poges, so far unidentified. The latest is almost certainly at Eton College, for the Rev. Montagu Rhodes James, Provost from 1918 to 1936, better known as M. R. James, the author of perhaps the best ghost stories ever written. There are two other twentieth century hatchments, for another Eton provost, James John Hornby, who died in 1909, and for William Lowndes, who died in 1905 at Chesham. The largest number in any one church is at Stoke Poges, where there are nineteen, only exceeded by the twenty at Wycombe Abbey. Those at Stoke Poges include the one already mentioned, and a number for members of the Penn family, one being for Thomas Penn, second son of William Penn, the founder of Pennsylvania. It is not often that one finds the hatchment of a Scottish laird in an English church, but the hatchment of Donald Cameron of Lochiel, 23rd chief of the clan, hangs in the church at Great Hampden. At Penn near-by are several hatchments of the Curzons, whose supporters are basilisks, those curious creatures who have additional heads at the end of their tails; and the hatchment of Francis, 2nd Viscount Lake at Aston Clinton bears a strange augmentation for his victory over the Maharatas, which consists of an argent chief charged with the Mahi Maratib surmounting the Goog and Ullum in saltire! It seems probable that all the hatchments now at Wycombe Abbey came originally from the parish church, perhaps at a time of restoration; certainly most of them, including some which have not been fully identified, belong to families associated with the town.

There are several interesting seventeenth century armorial boards, at Little Brickhill, Chalfont St Giles, and Langley Marish, all bearing inscriptions; these are rectangular, but another, at Medmenham, is very much a borderline example. It is of diamond shape, and bears the arms of Danvers on a lozenge: it is very small, only about a foot square, excluding the frame which is decorated with skulls and crossbones. It is kept out of the main text only because it bears the inscription, 'Neare this place lyeth ye Body of Mis Anne Danvers Obiit ye 21th Feb: 1677'; and this makes it clear that it is intended as a simple form of memorial. Details of these panels and transitional forms of hatchments will be included in a final volume when the county series on hatchments is completed.

Peter Summers

ASTON CLINTON

1. Dexter background black
Qly, 1st, Or an eagle displayed sable beaked gules, 2nd, Azure an arm embowed issuing from the sinister the hand grasping a sheaf of five arrows points downwards argent, 3rd, as 2nd but arm from dexter, 4th, Or a lion rampant proper; over all an escutcheon gules charged with a round target argent (Rothschild), in centre chief the Badge of Ulster, impaling, Argent a cedar tree between mounts proper, on a chief azure a dagger erect proper pommel and hilt or between two molets of six points or (Montefiore)   Austrian baron's coronet   Crests: 1. From a ducal coronet or a molet of six points or between two buffalo horns the dexter per fess or and sable the sinister per fess sable and or 2. From a ducal coronet or an eagle displayed sable   3. From a ducal coronet or three ostrich feathers, one argent between two azure   Motto: Concordia integritas industria   Supporters: Dexter, A lion rampant or   Sinister, A unicorn argent armed or
For Sir Anthony Rothschild, Bt., Baron of the Austrian Empire, cr. a baronet 1846, m. 1840, Louisa, dau. of Abraham Montefiore, and d. 4 Jan. 1876. (Foster's Peerage 1880 ed.)

2. Dexter background black
Azure a bend between six cross crosslets fitchy argent, on a chief of Augmentation argent, the fish of Mogul barways, per pale or and vert, banded vert and gules, pierced with a shaft erect headed with a crescent and by other shafts in saltire, headed with golden balls, an annulet, etc. (Lake), impaling, Argent a fess gules between six choughs proper (Onslow)   Viscount's coronet   Crest: A lion's head erased argent charged with a bar gemel gules   Supporters: Dexter, A Grenadier in uniform in the exterior hand a musket proper   Sinister: A Malay in uniform in the exterior hand a musket proper
For Francis, 2nd Viscount Lake, who m. Anne, dau. of Sir Richard Onslow, and d. 12 May 1836. (B.P. 1875 ed.; B.E.P.)

3. All black background
Qly, 1st and 4th, Azure a crescent argent between the horns an estoile or (Minshull), 2nd and 3rd, Sable a pile wavy argent (Rowland), impaling, Sable a chevron between in chief two bunches of grapes and in base a lion rampant or (Aufrere)
Crest: A Turk in armour proper habited gules wearing a turban, on bended knee, holding in the dexter hand a crescent argent
Mantling: Azure and argent   Motto: His saladinum vicimus armis
For George Rowland Minshull, Barrister-at-Law, who m. Louisa, dau.

of Anthony Aufrere, of Hoveton, Norfolk, and d. 6 July 1840.
She d. 1822. (B.L.G. 5th ed.)

4. Exactly similar to 3.

AYLESBURY, County Museum

1. **All black background**
On an asymmetric lozenge
Qly argent and gules four crosses formy counterchanged (Chetwode)
In pretence: Azure a chevron between three eagles' heads erased or langued gules (Aubrey)
For Elizabeth Sophia, widow of Charles Spencer Ricketts, and dau. of Thomas Aubrey, who m. 1868, as his 4th wife, the Rev. George Chetwode, of Chilton House, and d. 27 Nov. 1873. He d. 4 Aug. 1870. (B.P. 1949 ed.; M.I. in Boarstall church)

BIDDLESDEN

1. **Dexter background black**
Sable a lion rampant reguardant argent (Morgan), impaling, Ermine six lions rampant, three, two and one gules (Mabbott)
Crest: A demi-lion rampant reguardant argent   Mantling: Gules and argent   Motto: Resurgam
For George Morgan, who m. 1792, Frances, dau. of William Mabbott, of Bulmarsh, and d. 3 June 1819. (B.L.G. 5th ed.; M.I.)

2. **Dexter background black**
Morgan, impaling, Per saltire ermine and or on a chief per pale gules and sable three lions rampant reguardant argent collared or (Oliver)
Crest, mantling and motto: As 1.
For George Morgan, who m. 1820, Anna Elizabeth, dau. of George Oliver, of Brill Park, and d. 24 Dec. 1847, aged 53. (B.L.G. 5th ed.; M.I.)

BRADENHAM

1. **Sinister background black**
Gules a fess wavy between three fleurs-de-lys or (Hicks), impaling, Gules a fess vair between three unicorns statant argent (Wilkinson)
Motto: Mors janua vitæ   Cherub's head above
For Elizabeth, dau. of John Wilkinson, who m. as his 1st wife, John Hicks, of Bradenham, and d. June 1810. (M.I.; L.R. Muirhead; Par. regs.)

Buckinghamshire

2. Dexter background black
Hicks, impaling, Gules three lions rampant argent (   )
Crest: A stag's head couped or gorged with a wreath of laurel proper
Mantling: Gules and argent   Motto: Resurgam
For John Hicks, of Bradenham, who m. 2nd, Susanna Jemima Horlock, of Box, and d. 21 June 1823, aged 84. She d. 23 May 1845. (Sources, as 1.)

BROUGHTON

1. Dexter background black
Per chevron engrailed argent and gules three talbots' heads erased counterchanged (Duncombe), impaling, Sable a dove argent between three estoiles and a bordure engrailed or (Baron)
Crest: From a ducal coronet or a horse's hind leg sable shod argent
Mantling: Gules and argent   Cherub's head below   Frame decorated with skulls
For Francis Duncombe, who m. 1st, Mary, dau. of Sir Anthony Chester, and 2nd, Frances, dau. of James Baron, and d. 31 Jan. 1720. (M.I.)

CHALFONT ST GILES

1. All black background
Qly, 1st, Argent two bends engrailed sable (Radcliffe), 2nd, Azure two bars argent over all a bend gules (Lee), 3rd, Gules three cross crosslets fitchy and a chief or (Arderne), 4th, Azure a fess gules between three garbs or (Sambach)
Crest: A bull's head erased sable, armed, collared and chained argent
Mantling: Gules and argent   Motto: Mors janua vitæ
For Anthony Radcliffe, who was bur. 9 Dec. 1718. (Church guide)

2. Dexter background black
Argent a lion rampant gules between three trefoils slipped sable (Molloy), impaling, Argent on a fess engrailed azure three molets or within a bordure engrailed gules (Mure)
Crest: On a mound vert a greyhound courant argent in front of a tree proper   Mantling: Gules and argent   Motto: In coelo quies
For Charles Molloy, who m. Katherine, dau. of Hutchinson Mure, of Great Saxham, Suffolk, and d. 9 Apr. 1805, aged 57. She d. 30 July 1817, aged 60. (M.I.; Church guide)

3. Dexter background black
Per bend sinister or and sable six martlets counterchanged (Allen), impaling, Argent on a chevron between three griffins' heads erased sable three cinquefoils or (Jackson)

Crest: A martlet, in its beak an ear of corn, or   Mantling: Gules and argent   Motto: Resurgam
For Thomas Allen, of the Vache, who m. Sarah, dau. of William Jackson, of Tamworth, Staffs, and d. 18 Nov. 1829, aged 78. (M.I., Church guide)

4. **All black background**
On a lozenge   Arms: As 3.
Cherub's head above
For Sarah, widow of Thomas Allen. She d.   (Church guide)

5. **Dexter background black**
Vert a chevron argent between three wolves' heads erased or (Jones)   In pretence: Azure a cross formy fitchy or, on a chief ermine three covered cups gules (Eldred?) (The maiden name of the mother of the Rev. William Jones was Eldridge).   Also impaling, Argent a lion rampant gules between three fleurs-de-lys sable (Molloy)
Crest: A demi-lion rampant or, in its dexter paw a cross crosslet fitchy sable   Mantling: Gules and argent   Motto: Resurgam
For the Rev. William Jones, who m. 1806, Mary, only dau. of Charles Molloy, and d. 28 Jan. 1837, aged 68. She d. 5 Dec. 1847, aged 72. (M.I.; Church guide)

6. **Dexter background black**
Qly, 1st and 4th, Gules on a chevron between three towers argent issuant from each a demi-lion rampant or three grappling irons sable (Priestley), 2nd and 3rd, Argent a chevron engrailed sable between three leopards' faces azure (Copleston)   In pretence: Argent on a fess engrailed gules plain cotised sable between three lions rampant gules three bezants (Kirkman)   Crest: A cockatrice proper standing on a broken spear in fess holding in the beak the head or   Mantling: Gules and argent   Motto: Time Deum   Skull and crossbones below
For George Priestley, who m. 1819, Hannah, only dau. and heir of Nathaniel Kirkman, and d. 1 April 1849. She d. 4 Feb. 1871, aged 80. (B.L.G. 3rd ed.: Church guide: Par. regs.)

7. **All black background**
Argent a lion rampant sable langued gules within a bordure engrailed gules (Pomeroy)
Crest: A fircone vert charged with a bezant   Mantling: Gules and argent   Motto: Resurgam
For Henry William Pomeroy, of Little Chalfont, who d. 1824 or 1825, will proved 24 Mar. 1825. (Church guide)

8. **Sinister background black**
Qly, 1st and 4th, Gules two bars or a chief indented argent (Hare), 2nd, Azure ten molets of six points, four, three, two and one or (Alston),

3rd, Argent three bulls' heads erased sable (Trumbull), impaling, Ermine on a bend sable three eagles displayed or (Selman)
Motto: In coelo quies   Cherub's head above   Skull below
For Sarah, dau. and co-heir of Lister Selman, of Chalfont House, who m. as his 1st wife, the Rev. Robert Hare, of the Vache, Canon of Winchester, and d. 4 Sept. 1763, aged 29. (B.L.G. 7th ed.; Church guide; M.I.)

9. All black background
Per pale sable and argent three lions rampant counterchanged, in centre chief the Badge of Ulster (Palliser)
Crest: From a ducal coronet or a demi-eagle displayed or
Mantling: Gules and argent   Motto: In coelo quies
Four flags in saltire at base of shield.
For Sir Hugh Palliser, 1st Bt., Admiral of the White, of the Vache, who d. unm. 19 Mar. 1796, aged 74. (Source, as 8.)

CHALFONT ST PETER

1. Dexter background black
Gules a bowman in armour drawing a bow with arrow to sinister all proper (O'Loghlin), impaling, Azure a chevron or between in centre chief a pile or between two molets argent and in base a lion passant argent (Du Pré)
Crest: An anchor sable corded or   Mantling: Gules and argent
Motto: Armis vivo   Blue ensign and two others to dexter, red ensign and two others to sinister
For General Terence O'Loghlin, of Chalfont Grange, who m. Sophia Du Pré, of Wilton Park, Beaconsfield, and d. 11 Aug. 1843, aged 79. She d. 10 May 1861, aged 90. (M.I.; B.L.G. 1937 ed.)

2. Sinister background black
Azure three horses' heads couped argent bridled gules (Chevall), impaling, Gules a lion rampant between three cross crosslets fitchy or (Capel)   Motto: In coelo quies   Cherub's head above
Unidentified

3. All black background
Per chevron sable and argent three elephants' heads erased counterchanged (Saunders), impaling. Or on a fess dancetty azure between three escutcheons azure each charged with a lion rampant or three bezants (Rolls)
Crest; An elephant's head proper   Mantling: Gules and argent
Motto: Mors janua vitæ
For Sir Thomas Saunders, who m. 1688, Jane Rolls, and d. (Par. Regs.)

4. Dexter background black
Gules on a chevron argent between three hawks close proper three cross crosslets fitchy gules, on a chief ermine three demi-spears erect sable points embrued gules (Gaskell), impaling, Argent a lion rampant sable langued gules (? Stapleton)
Crest: At the foot of a tree proper on a mound vert a greyhound courant sable collared or the dexter paw supporting an escutcheon or charged with a fleur-de-lys azure   Mantling: Gules and argent
Motto: In coelo quies
For Capt. William Gaskell, who m. Elizabeth, and d. 25 May 1822, aged 66. She d. 10 Jan. 1840, aged 71. (M.I.)

5. Dexter background black
Or a chevron ermine between three leaves erect vert (? Burwell)   In pretence: Vert a fess dancetty and in chief three garbs or (Wheate)
Crest: A lion's head erased or in its mouth an oak sprig proper
Mantling: Gules and argent   Motto: Mors janua vitæ
Unidentified

6. Dexter background black
Ermine on a bend sable three crescents argent (Hibbert), impaling, Sable a fess chequy argent and azure (   )
Crest: A cubit arm erect vested azure cuffed argent the hand proper holding a crescent argent   Mantling: Gules and argent
Motto: Fidem rectumque colindo
Unidentified

7. All black background
On a lozenge surmounted by a cherub's head
Hibbert, impaling, Per pale or and azure a saltire counterchanged charged with another couped and counterchanged (Boldero)
Motto: Resurgam
For Sophia Boldero, of London, who m. Thomas Hibbert, of Chalfont Park, and d. 17 Feb. 1827, aged 67. He d. 25 May 1819. (M.I.)

CHENIES

The majority of these hatchments are not original. Some are probably replacements, and others have been repainted. Nos. 6, 8 and 9, for Russells who died in 1808, 1874 and 1891, were certainly all painted at the same time being identical in style and finish.

1. All black background
Within the Garter, Argent a lion rampant gules on a chief sable three escallops argent (Russell), impaling, Gules on a chevron argent three molets sable in chief a lion passant guardant or (Carr)

Buckinghamshire 51

Duke's coronet   Crest: A goat passant argent armed and unguled or
Mantling: Gules and argent   Motto: Che sara sara   Supporters:
Dexter, A lion rampant gules   Sinister, A goat gules, armed, unguled
and tufted, ducally gorged and chained or
For William, 1st Duke of Bedford, K.G., who m. 1637, Anne, dau. and
sole heiress of Robert Carr, Earl of Somerset, and d. 7 Sept. 1700.
(B.P. 1949 ed.)   Not contemporary; probably a replacement.

2. All black background
Russell, impaling, Qly, 1st and 4th, Barry of eight argent and gules a
cross moline sable (Gower), 2nd and 3rd, Azure three laurel leaves
erect or (Leveson)
Duchess's coronet   Supporters: Dexter, A lion rampant gules
Sinister, A ? lioness argent (should be wolf) collared and chained or
For Gertrude, elder dau. of John, 1st Earl Gower, who m. 1737, as his
2nd wife, John, 4th Duke of Bedford, K.G., and d. 1 July 1794.
(B.P. 1949 ed.)

3. Dexter background black
Russell, with label argent for difference, impaling, Gules three
escallops argent (Keppel)
Marquess's coronet   Crest: A goat passant argent, armed and unguled
or   Motto: Che sara sara   Supporters: Dexter, A lion rampant gules
Sinister, A lion rampant or
For Francis, Marquess of Tavistock, who m. 1764, Elizabeth, dau. of
William, 2nd Earl of Albemarle, and d. 22 Mar. 1767. (B.P. 1949 ed.)

4. All black background
On a lozenge   Russell, with chief gules, and label argent for
difference, impaling, Keppel
Marchioness's coronet   Motto and supporters: As 3.
For Elizabeth, widow of Francis, Marquess of Tavistock. She d. 2 Nov.
1768.
(B.P. 1949 ed.)

5. Sinister background black
Russell, with crescent argent for difference, impaling, Qly sable and
argent in the first quarter a lion rampant argent langued gules (Byng)
Supporters: As 1., but antelope instead of goat   Shield suspended
from a bow of ribbons
For Georgiana Elizabeth, dau. of George, 4th Viscount Torrington,
who m. 1786, as his 1st wife, Lord John Russell, later 6th Duke of
Bedford, K.G., and d. 11 Oct. 1801. (B.P. 1949 ed.)

6. Sinister background black
Russell, impaling, Argent on a cross gules five escallops or (Villiers)
For Charlotte Anne, eldest dau. of George, 4th Earl of Jersey, who

m. 1789, Lord William Russell, son of Francis, Marquess of Tavistock, and d. 31 Aug. 1808. (B.P. 1949 ed.)
(There is another hatchment for Lady Charlotte Russell at Woburn Abbey)

7. **Dexter background black**
Russell, with a molet argent on a molet gules for difference   In pretence; Qly, 1st and 4th, Chequy or and azure a fess gules (Clifford), 2nd and 3rd, Azure on a chevron between three molets or three trefoils slipped vert (Coussmaker)
Crest, mantling and motto: As 1.
For Commander John Russell, son of Lord William Russell, who m. 1822, Sophia, Baroness de Clifford, dau. of Col. George Coussmaker, and d. 27 Apr. 1835. (B.P. 1949 ed.)

8. **All black background**
Russell   In pretence: Qly, 1st, Argent a fess between three pheons sable (Rawdon), 2nd, Argent a maunch sable (Hastings), 3rd, Per pale or and sable a saltire engrailed counterchanged (Pole), 4th, Qly France and England a label of three points argent (Plantagenet)
For Elizabeth Anne, only child of the Hon. John Theophilus Rawdon, who m. 1817, General Lord George William Russell, and d. 10 Aug. 1874; or for her husband, who d. 16 July 1846. (B.P. 1949 ed.)

9. **Dexter background black**
Russell, impaling, Qly, 1st and 4th, Argent a fess dancetty sable (West), 2nd and 3rd, Qly or and gules over all a bend vair (Sackville)
No crest, mantling, supporters, etc. Space between shield and frame filled with ornamental scrollwork. Identical in this respect to Nos. 6. and 8.
For Francis Charles Hastings, 9th Duke of Bedford, K.G., who m. 1844, Elizabeth, dau. of George John, 5th Earl de la Warr, and d. 14 Jan. 1891. (B.P. 1949 ed.)

10. **All black background**
Russell arms only
Duke's coronet   Crest, mantling and motto: As 1.   Supporters: Dexter, A lion rampant gules collared argent the collar charged with three escallops sable   Sinister, A goat argent, armed, unguled and tufted, ducally gorged and chained or
For Hastings William Sackville, 12th Duke of Bedford, who m. 1914, Louisa, younger dau. of Robert Jowitt Whitwell, of Thornbury Lodge, Oxford, and d. 9 Oct. 1953. (B.P. 1970 ed.)

Buckinghamshire

CHEQUERS

1. All black background
Qly. 1st and 4th, Argent a lion rampant gules langued azure, on a chief sable three roses argent barbed vert (Russell), 2nd, Vert two bars and in chief a lion passant argent (Greenhill), 3rd, Or on a chief gules a lion passant or (Noble), over all the Badge of Ulster
Crests: Dexter, A goat passant argent ducally gorged armed and unguled or   Sinister, A demi-griffin segreant or   Mantling: Gules and argent   Motto: Resurgam
For Sir Robert Greenhill-Russell, Bt., who d. unm. 1837.   Robert Greenhill, Esq., of Chequers Court, assumed by sign manual in 1815 the name and arms of Russell, and was created a baronet in 1831. On his death the baronetcy expired and the estate devolved on his kinsman, Sir Robert Frankland, Bt., who assumed the additional name of Russell. (B.E.B.)

2. Dexter background black
Qly, 1st and 4th, Azure a dolphin embowed argent finned gules, on a chief or two saltires gules (Frankland), 2nd and 3rd, Argent a lion rampant gules langued azure, on a chief sable three roses argent barbed and seeded proper (Russell), over all the Badge of Ulster, impaling, Qly of eight, 1st, Azure three molets within a double tressure flory counterflory or (Murray), 2nd, Gules three legs in armour proper garnished and spurred or conjoined in triangle (Isle of Man), 3rd, Gules two lions passant guardant in pale argent (Strange), 4th, Argent on a bend azure three stags' heads cabossed or (Stanley), 5th, Or a fess chequy azure and argent (Stewart), 6th, Paly of eight or and sable (Atholl), 7th, Gules three cinquefoils argent (Hamilton), 8th, Qly France and England
Crests: Dexter, A dolphin hauriant vert finned gules entwined round an anchor erect proper   Sinister, A goat passant argent, murally gorged and armed or   Mantling: Gules and argent   Motto: Know Thyself
For Sir Robert Frankland-Russell, 7th Bt., who m. 1815, Louisa Anne (d. 21 Feb. 1871), 3rd dau. of the Rt. Rev. Lord George Murray, Bishop of St Davids, and d. 11 Mar. 1849. Sir Robert inherited from the Russell family Chequers Court, and assumed by sign manual, 1837, the surname of Russell, in addition to and after that of Frankland. (B.P. 1965 ed.)

(These hatchments are not at any time on view to the general public)

CHESHAM

1. Sinister background black
Argent fretty azure each interlacing charged with a bezant, on a canton gules a leopard's head erased or, a molet sable for difference (Lowndes),

impaling, Gules six escallops, three, two and one argent (Shales)
Crest: A leopard's head erased or gorged with a laurel branch proper
Mantling: Gules and argent   Motto: Mors janua vitæ
For Anne, eldest dau. and co-heir of Charles Shales, who m. 1730,
Charles Lowndes, of Chesham, Secretary of the Treasury, and was bur.
1 Mar. 1759, aged 59. He d. 31 Mar. 1783, aged 83. (B.L.G. 1937 ed.;
Par. regs.)

2. All black background
Lowndes (no molet), impaling, Argent a bend between two lions
rampant sable (Osborne)
Crest and mantling: As 1.   Motto: Resurgam
For William Lowndes, of Chesham, Commissioner of Excise, who m.
1771, Lydia Mary, dau. of Robert Osborne, Commissioner of the Navy,
and was bur. 7 May 1808. (Sources, as 1.)

3. Dexter background black
Argent fretty azure each interlacing charged with a bezant, on a canton
gules a leopard's head erased or langued azure gorged with a laurel
branch proper (Lowndes), impaling, Gules a cross or between four
leopards' faces argent (Kingston)
Crest: A leopard's head erased or langued gules gorged with a laurel
branch proper   Mantling and motto: As 2.
For William Lowndes, of Chesham, J.P & D.L., who m. 1803, Harriet
Wilson, dau. of John Kingston, of Rickmansworth, and was bur. 9 July
1831. (Sources, as 1.)

4. All black background
On a lozenge surmounted by a cherub's head
Arms: As 3.   Motto: Resurgam
For Harriet Wilson, widow of William Lowndes. She was bur. 12 Feb.
1848, aged 65. (Sources, as 1.)

5. Sinister background black
Argent fretty azure each interlacing charged with a bezant, on a canton
gules a leopard's head erased or gorged with a laurel branch proper
(Lowndes), impaling, Qly, 1st and 4th, Azure a double-headed lion
rampant argent holding between its paws a crescent or (Mason), 2nd
and 3rd, Argent a lion rampant sable langued gules within a bordure
engrailed gules (Pomeroy)   On a shield suspended from blue ribbons
and with a cherub's head at each top angle   Motto: Resurgam
For Mary Harriet, 3rd dau. of Kender Mason of Amersham, who m.
1830, as his 1st wife, William Lowndes, and d. 18 Apr. 1836. (B.L.G.
1937 ed.)

6. Dexter background black
Lowndes, as 3., impaling to dexter, Qly, 1st and 4th, Mason, 2nd and
3rd, Pomeroy, and to sinister, Argent a canton sable (Sutton)

Crest: As 3.   Mantling: Azure and argent   Motto: Ways and means
For William Lowndes, who m. 1st, 1830, Mary Harriet, 3rd dau. of
Kender Mason of Amersham, and 2nd, 1837, Martha, 3rd dau. of
Robert Sutton, of Rossway, and d. Aug. 1864. (B.L.G. 1937 ed.)

7. All black background
Lowndes, as 3.
Crest, mantling and motto: As 6.
Probably for William Lowndes, J.P. & D.L., who d unm. 12 Nov.
1905. (B.L.G. 1937 ed.)

8. Dexter background black
Argent three bears' heads erased sable muzzled gules (Barwicke),
impaling, Gules a saltire engrailed argent (   )
Crest: An escarbuncle argent   Mantling: Gules and argent
Motto: Mors janua vitæ   Skull below
Possibly for Newe Barwick, of Chesham, who d. 26 Feb. 1780.
(Gents. Mag. 1780, p. 154)

9. Dexter background black
Per fess or and azure a molet of eight points counterchanged
(Skottowe), impaling, Paly of six or and gules a bend argent
(Langford)
Crest: A cubit arm erect vested azure cuffed argent the hand proper
holding a molet of eight points per fess azure and or   Mantling: Gules
and argent   Motto: In coelo quies
For Coulson Skottowe, of Chesham, High Sheriff of Bucks, who m.
Anne Langford, and d. 21 Apr. 1784. (Franks Cat. of Bookplates;
Skottowe family history; M.I.)

10. All black background
On a lozenge surmounted by a cherub's head
Arms: As 9   Motto: Mori lucrum   Skull below
For the widow of Coulson Skottowe. She d. 16 July 1784.
(Sources, as 9.)

CHESHAM BOIS

1. Dexter background black
Argent three bars and a canton gules (Fuller), impaling, Argent on a
cross sable five bezants (Stratton)
Crest: A beacon fired proper   Mantling: Gules and argent
Motto: Firmiora futura
For Benjamin Fuller, of Hyde House and Germans, Chesham, who m.
Charlotte (d. 26 May 1889), dau. of John Stratton, of Little
Berkhamstead, and d. 20 Mar. 1882, aged 90. (M.I. in churchyard)

2. Dexter background black
Fuller, impaling, Azure a lion rampant argent, over all a bend gules charged with three escallops argent (Taylor)
Crest, mantling and motto: As 1.
For John Stratton Fuller (son of 1.), who m. Elizabeth Juliana (d. 26 Jan. 1892), and d. 23 Jan. 1892, aged 48. (Source, as 1.)

CHETWODE

1. Dexter background black
Argent a fess azure between three crescents gules (Risley), impaling, Per chevron engrailed gules and argent three talbots' heads erased counterchanged (Duncombe)
Crest: A greyhound statant ermine collared or its dexter paw resting upon an escutcheon argent   Mantling: Gules and argent   Motto: Dulce et decorum est pro patria mori
For Henry Risley, who m. Elizabeth Duncombe and was killed in action at Brest,   (Lipscombe, iii. 3)

2. All black background
On a lozenge surmounted by cherubs' heads
Arms: As 1.   Skull below
For Elizabeth, widow of Henry Risley. She d. (Source, as 1.)

3. All black background
Risley arms only   Crest and mantling: As 1.   Motto: Ictus non victus
For Paul Risley, son of Henry Risley, who d. unm. 20 Feb. 1738, aged 68. (Source, as 1.)

4. Dexter background black
Risley   In pretence: Sable a fess between three mascles argent (Whitaker)   Crest and mantling: As 1.   Motto: Resurgemus
Skull below
For Risley Risley (né Brewer), heir to his uncle, Paul Risley. He m. Ann, dau. of Sir Edward Whitaker, and d. 15 Nov. 1755. (Source, as 1.)

CLIFTON REYNES

1. All black background
Sable on a bend argent three roses gules barbed vert in sinister chief a tower argent (Small)
Crest: A tower argent   Mantling: Gules and argent   Motto: Resurgam   On background in base: A. S. Esqr. 1816.
For Alexander Small, of Clifton Hall, Physician to George III, who d. 19 Aug. 1816, aged 68. (M.I.)

Buckinghamshire

DINTON

1. All black background
Qly, 1st, Or two olive branches in saltire proper (Vanhattem), 2nd, Sable a chevron or and in base a hind lodged argent (   ), 3rd, Sable a chevron or between three birds argent beaked and legged or (   ), 4th, Gules a lion rampant between eight fleurs-de-lys argent (Davall)
Crest: A hind's head between two olive branches proper
No mantling, but decorative scrollwork   Motto: Non omnis moriar
Skull below
For Sir John Vanhattem, of Dinton Hall, who d. 4 Dec. 1787. (M.I.)

2. Dexter background black
Gules an eagle displayed argent, on a canton or a chaplet graminy vert (Goodall)   In pretence: Qly, 1st, Vanhattem, 2nd, Sable a chevron or and in a base a hind lodged proper (   ), 3rd, Sable a chevron or between three ducks proper beaked and legged or (   ), 4th, Gules a lion rampant between eight fleurs-de-lys argent (Davall)
Crest: An eagle displayed argent armed or   Mantling: Gules and argent   Motto: Constantia
For the Rev. William Goodall, of Dinton Hall, who m. 1788, Rebecca, dau. of Sir John Vanhattem, and d. 10 Jan. 1844. (B.L.G. 5th ed.; L. R. Muirhead)

3. All black background
On a lozenge surmounted by a cherub's head
Goodall, impaling, Qly, 1st, Vanhattem, 2nd, Sable a chevron or and in base a hind lodged argent (   ), 3rd, Sable a chevron or between three birds argent beaked and legged or (   ), 4th, Gules a lion rampant between eight fleurs-de-lys argent (Davall)
Motto: Resurgam
For Rebecca, widow of the Rev. William Goodall. She d. 13 Oct. 1853. (B.L.G. 5th ed.; MS Book of Dinton)

DORNEY

1. All black background
Or two bars gules each charged with three trefoils slipped argent, in chief a greyhound courant sable, in fess point the Badge of Ulster (Palmer)
Crest: A demi-panther guardant argent semy of roundels azure holding in its paws a palm branch proper   Mantling: Gules and or   Motto: Palma virtuti   Supporters: Two lions rampant guardant argent
For Sir Charles Harcourt Palmer, 6th Bt. of Dorney Court, who d. 19 Feb. 1838. (Lt.-Col. P. D. S. Palmer)

2. Dexter background black
Palmer, impaling, Azure a lion rampant guardant ermine ducally crowned or (Gerrard)
Crest: A demi-panther guardant flames issuant from mouth and ears, holding in its paws a palm branch proper   Motto: Palma virtuti
Supporters: Two lions rampant guardant or
For the Rev. Henry Palmer, who m. 1827, Sarah, dau. of George Gerrard, of Burnham, Bucks, and d. 20 Nov. 1865. (Lt.-Col. P. D. S. Palmer)

ETON College

1. Sinister background black
Sable three lily flowers argent, on a chief per pale azure and gules a fleur-de-lys and a lion passant guardant or (Eton College), impaling, Or two chevrons between three bugle horns sable stringed gules, on a chief sable three eagles' legs erased or (Hornby)
In a heavy glazed frame
For the Rev. James John Hornby, D.D., Provost 1884–1909, who d. 2 Nov. 1909. (per Librarian)

2. All black background
Sable on a chevron between three lions passant guardant or three escallops gules (James)
Crest: A demi-lion rampant or langued gules holding between its paws an escallop gules   Mantling: Grey and argent   Motto: Resurgam
For the Rev. Montague Rhodes James, O.M., Provost 1918-1936, who d. 12 June 1936. (per Librarian)

FULMER

1. All black background
Argent two bends sable (Kaye), impaling, Azure two swans argent between two flaunches ermine (Mellish)
Crest: A griffin's head erased ermine holding in its beak a key or
Mantling: Gules and argent   Motto: Kynd kynn knawne keppe
For John Kaye, J.P., High Sheriff of Middlesex, who m. Catherine (Mellish), and d. 12 Aug. 1861, aged 82. She d. 28 Oct. 1859, aged 81. (M.I.)

2. Dexter background black
Qly, 1st and 4th, Sable a cross engrailed or, 2nd and 3rd, Gules a cross botonny argent, all within a bordure compony argent and gules, over all the Badge of Ulster (Willoughby), impaling, Azure three bends or a chief ermine (Hawkes)

Buckinghamshire

Crest: A Saracen's bust affronté couped at the shoulders proper ducally crowned or   Mantling: Gules and argent   Motto: Verité sans peur
For Sir John Pollard Willoughby, 4th Bt., M.P., who m. 2nd, 1854, Maria Elizabeth, 4th dau. of Thomas Hawkes, of Himley House, Staffs, and d. 15 Sept. 1866. (B.P. 1868 ed.)

GAYHURST

1. Sinister background black
Qly, 1st and 4th, Azure two bars engrailed and in chief three leopards' faces argent (Wrighte), 2nd, Argent a chevron between three towers sable (Oneby), 3rd, Argent three lions' gambs erased within a bordure engrailed sable (Bedford)   In pretence: Argent a fess between three hinds trippant sable (Jekyll)   Motto: In coelo quies   Shield suspended from a bow of blue ribbon   Cherubs' heads at sides
For Anne, dau. and heir of Joseph Jekyll, of Dallington, Northants, who m. George Wrighte, of Gayhurst, and d. 5 Dec. 1789. (Burke's Commoners, Vol. II)

2. All black background
Arms: As 1.
Crest: A dragon's head erased or collared azure   Mantling: Gules and argent   Motto: Resurgam
For George Wrighte, who m. Anne, dau. and heir of Joseph Jekyll, and d. 1804. (Lipscombe, iv, 151)

3. All black background
On a lozenge surmounted by a cherub's head
Qly, of six, 1st, Azure two bars engrailed argent and in chief three leopards' faces or (Wrighte), 2nd, Or a chevron vert between three towers gules (Oneby), 3rd, Bedford, 4th, Jekyll, 5th, Argent three fusils conjoined in fess gules within a bordure sable (Montagu), 6th, Or an eagle displayed vert (Monthermer)
For Anne, only surviving child of George Wrighte and Anne Jekyll; she d. 19 Jan. 1830, aged 46. (Burke's Commoners; M.I.)

4. Dexter three-quarters background black
Qly, 1st and 4th, Argent a cross gules between four peacocks azure (Carrington), 2nd, Argent on a bend sable three pairs of falchions in saltire argent (Smith), 3rd, Or a chevron cotised between three demi-griffins couped the two in chief respectant sable (Smith), impaling two coats to the sinister, first, Qly per fess indented argent and sable in the first and fourth quarters a bugle horn stringed sable garnished or (Forester), and second, Qly, 1st and 4th, Or fretty azure (Willoughby), 2nd and 3rd, Or three bars wavy gules (Drummond)

Baron's coronet   Crests: Dexter, A peacock's head erased azure beaked and ducally gorged or   Sinister, An elephant's head erased or charged with three fleurs-de-lys azure   Supporters: Dexter, A griffin sable winged and beaked or, charged with three fleurs-de-lys or Sinister, A lion gules gutty or   Motto: Regi semper fidelis
For Robert John Smith, 2nd Baron Carrington, who m. 1st, 1822, Elizabeth Catherine, dau. of Cecil, 1st Baron Forester, and 2nd, 1840, Charlotte Augusta Annabella, dau. of Peter, Baron Willoughby de Eresby, and d. 17 Mar. 1868. She d. 26 July 1879.   (B.P. 1949 ed.)

HAMBLEDON

1. All black background
Argent on a chief gules a cushion argent between two molets or, a martlet sable for difference (Marjoribanks), impaling, Or ermined sable a fess embattled plain cotised gules in chief a turret sable (Lautour) Crest: A lion's gamb erased argent holding a lance or   Mantling: Gules and argent   Motto: Requiescat in pace
For Edward Marjoribanks, of Greenlands, Bucks, who m. 1808, Georgiana, 3rd dau. of Joseph Francis Louis Latour, and d. 17 Sept. 1868. She d. 17 Apr. 1849. (B.P. 1868 ed.)

GREAT HAMPDEN

1. Dexter background black
Two shields   Dexter, within Order of Hanover, Qly, 1st and 4th, Argent a saltire gules between four eagles displayed azure (Hampden), 2nd and 3rd, Per bend sinister ermine and or ermined sable a lion rampant or (Trevor)   Sinister, within a wreath, Gules on a chevron between three fleurs-de-lys or a crescent between two martlets sable (Brown)
Viscount's coronet   Crest: A talbot statant ermine collared and corded gules   Motto: Vestigia nulla retrorsum   Star of Order below dexter shield   All on a mantle gules and ermine
For Thomas, 2nd Viscount Hampden, who m. 1st, Catherine (d. 1804), dau. of Gen. David Graeme, and 2nd, Maria, dau. of John Brown of Elliston, Scotland, and d.s.p. 20 Aug. 1824. She d. 27 June 1833. (Complete Peerage)

2. Dexter background black
Two shields   Dexter, Qly, 1st and 4th, Hampden, 2nd and 3rd, Trevor   Sinister, Azure a cross engrailed between four cinquefoils argent (Burton)   Viscount's coronet   Crest and motto: As 1. Supporters: Two wyverns reguardant sable, winged, beaked and legged gules

For John, 3rd Viscount Hampden, who m. 1773, Harriet, only dau. of the Rev. Daniel Burton, Canon of Christ Church, and d.s.p. 9 Sept. 1824. (Source, as 1.)

3. Dexter background black
Qly, 1st and 4th, Hampden, 2nd and 3rd, Sable an estoile or between two flaunches ermine (Hobart)
Earl's coronet   Crests: Dexter, A talbot statant ermine collared and corded gules   Sinister, A bull per pale sable and gules bezanty
Mottoes: Vestigio nulla retrorsum   Auctor pretiosae facit
Supporters: Dexter, A stag reguardant proper gorged with a radiant collar corded or   Sinister, A talbot reguardant argent similarly collared and corded
For George Robert, 5th Earl of Buckinghamshire, who m. 1819, Anne Glover, dau. of Sir Arthur Pigot, and d. 1 Feb. 1849. (B.P. 1949 ed.)

4. All black background
Qly, 1st and 4th, Hampden, 2nd and 3rd, Hobart, impaling, in chief, Argent a lion passant between three fleurs-de-lys azure (Williams), and in base, Or a lion rampant azure charged with a fleur-de-lys or (Egremont)
Earl's coronet   Crests and supporters: As 3.   Motto: As 1.
For Augustus Edward, 6th Earl of Buckinghamshire, who m. 1st, 1816, Mary, eldest dau. of John Williams, King's Serjeant, and 2nd, 1826, Maria Isabella, dau. of the Rev. Godfrey Egremont, and d. 29 Oct. 1885. (B.P. 1949 ed.)

5. Dexter background black
Gules three bars or (Cameron), impaling, Hobart
Crest: An arm in armour embowed azure garnished or holding a sword argent hilted or   Motto: Pro rege et patria   Supporters: Two wild men girt at the loins with leaves and holding in their outer hands a Lochaber axe all proper
For Donald Cameron of Lochiel, D.L., 23rd chief, who m. 1832, Vere Catherine Louisa, dau. of the Hon. George Vere Hobart, and d. 2 Dec. 1858. (B.L.G. 1937 ed.)

HANSLOPE

1. All black background
Azure three arrows in fess points downwards or barbed and feathered argent, on a chief or three Moors' heads in profile couped sable (Watts)
Crest: A greyhound sejant argent supporting with its dexter paw an arrow erect point downwards or barbed and feathered argent
Mantling: Gules and argent   Motto: Non fecit mauri jaculis neque arcu
Probably for Edward Watts, who d. unm. 1800. (B.L.G. 1937 ed.)

2. Dexter background black

Watts, impaling, Argent on a fess gules three cross crosslets argent, on a canton azure five fleurs-de-lys, two, one, two or (Wynch)
Crest: A greyhound sejant argent collared or supporting with its dexter paw an arrow in bend point downwards or barbed and feathered argent
Mantling: Gules and argent   Motto: Resurgam
For Edward Watts, of Hanslope Park, who m. Florentina, dau. of Alexander Wynch, Governor of Fort St George, Madras, and d. 9 Apr. 1830, aged 79. (M.I.; B.L.G. 1937 ed.)

3. All black background

On a shield, not on a lozenge, surmounted by a cherub's head
Arms: As 2.   Motto: Resurgam
For Florentina, widow of Edward Watts. She d. 21 Feb. 1832, aged 71. (M.I.; B.L.G. 1937 ed.)

HITCHAM

1. Dexter background black

Qly, 1st and 4th, Or on a fess between two chevrons sable three cross crosslets or (Walpole), 2nd and 3rd, Azure a lion rampant or (Robsart), impaling, Per fess argent and gules a pale counterchanged, over all a lion rampant or ermined sable, on a canton azure five fleurs-de-lys two, one, two or (Hammet)
Crest: From a ducal coronet or a man's bust in profile proper wearing a cap gules   Mantling: Gules and argent   Motto: Fari quæ sentiat
For Richard Walpole, son of the Hon. Richard Walpole, who m. Elizabeth, dau. of Sir Benjamin Hammet, M.P. for Taunton, and d. 15 Aug. 1811, aged 49. (M.I.)

2. All black background

On a lozenge surmounted by a cherub's head
Arms: As 1.
For Elizabeth, widow of Richard Walpole. She d. 19 Mar. 1815, aged 43. (M.I.)

3. Dexter background black

Vert on a chevron between three stags trippant or three cinquefoils gules, the Badge of Ulster (Robinson), impaling, Qly argent and gules on the second and third a fret argent, over all on a bend sable three escallops argent (Spencer)
Crest: A stag trippant or   Mantling: Gules and argent
Motto: Solo in Deo salus
For the Rev. Sir John Robinson, 1st Bt., who m. 1786, Mary Anne, 2nd dau. of James Spencer, of Rathangan, co. Kildare, and d. 16 Apr. 1832. She d. 19 Jan. 1834. (B.P. 1878 ed.)

Buckinghamshire

4. All black background
On a lozenge surmounted by an escallop
Argent a lion rampant or, on a canton azure seven fleurs-de-lys two, two and three or (Hammet), impaling, Gules a lion's head erased between three molets of six points or (Esdaile)
For Louisa, dau. of Sir James Esdaile, who m. Sir Benjamin Hammet, M.P., for Taunton, and d. 16 Nov. 1816. (Burke's Commoners, Vol. 3, p. 604; M.I.)

5. All black background
On a lozenge surmounted by a cherub's head
Azure three molets argent, on a chief argent three bendlets sinister gules (Dickson)   In pretence: Argent three greyhounds courant in pale sable collared or (Moore)
For Susanna Jane, only dau. of Sir Henry Moore, Bt., who m. Col. A. Dickson and d. 15 Apr. 1821. (M.I.; Annual Register)

6. All black background
On a lozenge suspended from a lover's knot
Gules a chevron between in chief two cinquefoils and in base a bugle horn stringed or (Duncan), impaling, Or a cross potent quarter pierced azure between three molets pierced argent (Milne)
Motto: In coelo quies   Cherubs' heads at sides and below lozenge
No frame
Unidentified

LACEY GREEN

1. Dexter background black
Or three piles sable, on a chief or three annulets sable, in dexter chief the Badge of Ulster (Young), impaling, Azure on a fess between three ostrich feathers argent three martlets sable (Tufnell)
Crest: A cubit arm erect, the hand grasping an arrow proper
Mantling: Gules and argent   Motto: Press through
For Sir William Lawrence Young, 3rd Bt., who m. 1805, Anna Louisa (d. 4 Feb. 1844), 2nd dau. of William Tufnell, of Langleys, Essex, and d. 3 Nov. 1824. (B.P. 1949 ed.)

LANGLEY MARISH

1. Sinister background black
Gules on a chevron engrailed or between three swans argent three bees volant proper (Swabey), impaling, Argent a cross flory vert between four martlets gules, a chief dovetailed azure (Bird)

Motto: Resurgam   Shield flanked with leafy branches and suspended from a lover's knot.
For Catherine, dau. of Robert Bird, of Barton-on-the-Heath, Warwick, who m. 1783, as his first wife, Maurice Swabey, of Langley Marish, J.P., D.L. and d. 28 Jan. 1803. (B.L.G. 1937 ed.; M.I.)

2. **Dexter background black**
Qly, 1st and 4th, Swabey, 2nd and 3rd, Argent a chevron between three roses gules barbed and seeded proper (Birchfield), impaling, Ermine on a chevron engrailed sable between three molets azure three leopards' faces or (Creed)
Crest: A tower gules fired proper in front of three arrows one in fess point to the sinister, the others in saltire points downwards or
Mantling: Gules and or   Motto: Vera tropæa fides
For Maurice Swabey, who m. 2nd, 1804, Elizabeth, dau. of Edward Creed, of Cork, and d. 10 Feb. 1826. (Sources, as 1.)

3. **All gold background**
On a lozenge   Arms: As 2.
A very small hatchment
For Elizabeth, widow of Maurice Swabey. She d.   (Sources, as 1.)

4. **Sinister background black**
Qly, as 2., impaling, Qly, 1st, Vert on a chevron between three unicorns' heads erased or three crescents gules (Clowes), 2nd, Argent five lozenges conjoined in pale sable (Daniell), 3rd, Argent a wolf statant reguardant sable (Daniell), 4th, Azure a chevron ermine between three arrows or barbed and feathered argent, on a chief argent three choughs proper, and on a canton gules a molet or (Dawson)
Motto: Resurgam
For Frances, only dau. of Charles Clowes, who m. Maurice Swabey, of Langley Marish, J.P., D.L., and d. 11 May 1859, aged 76. (Sources, as 1.)

5. **All black background**
On a lozenge surmounted by a cherub's head
Gules a chevron between three crescents or (Gosling)   In pretence:
Qly, 1st and 4th, Argent three bars azure (Houghton), 2nd and 3rd, Argent three lions passant guardant in pale gules (Brograve)
For Elizabeth, dau. of William Houghton, who m. Robert Gosling, of Hassobury, Essex, and d. 6 June 1811, aged 68. (Sources, as 1.)

6. **Sinister background black**
Qly, 1st and 4th, Gules a chevron between three crescents or (Gosling), 2nd and 3rd, qly. i. & iv. Argent three bars azure (Houghton), ii. & iii. Argent three lions passant guardant in pale gules (Brograve)

In pretence: Qly, 1st and 4th, Sable three conies argent (Cunliffe), 2nd and 3rd, indistinguishable
Motto: Resurgam Cherub's head above and leafy branches flanking shield A small hatchment in poor condition, argent is now sable, and the canvas is torn.
For Margaret Elizabeth, dau. and co-heir of Sir Ellis Cunliffe, Bt., of Acton, Cheshire, who m. as his first wife, William Gosling, of Roehampton, and d. 18 Dec. 1803. (Sources, as 1.)

7. All black background
Azure a garb or between three bezants (Grosvenor) To dexter of main shield, Grosvenor, impaling, Chequy argent and sable (   ) A.B1.
To sinister of main shield, Grosvenor, impaling, Or a chevron gules between three lions' gambs erased sable (Austen) A.B1.
Helm, but no crest Mantling: Gules and argent Motto: In coelo quies
Probably for Sherrington Grosvenor, who d. 4 Apr. 1786. His wife, Finetta, d. 4 Mar. 1771. (Par. regs.)

THE LEE (old church)

1. All black background
Gules a lion rampant argent over all two bendlets or (Plaistowe)
Motto: Memento mori Two cherubs' heads above and skull below
Unidentified

LILLINGSTONE LOVEL

1. Dexter background black
Qly, 1st and 4th, Gules on a pile between two roses argent barbed vert a doubleheaded eagle displayed gules (Delap), 2nd and 3rd, Or a chevron vair between in chief two roses gules barbed and seeded proper and in base a ship in full sail sable (Bogle) In pretence: Qly of six, 1st, Azure a chevron argent between three molets or (Hillier), 2nd, Azure a fess argent between three leopards' faces per pale or and argent (? Newarke), 3rd, Argent a tower between three keys wards upwards and to dexter sable (Baker), 4th, Argent on a bend azure three lions passant or (   ), 5th, Azure three stags trippant or (Green), 6th, Azure a cross formy fitchy or, on a chief or three roundels azure (Eldred)
Crest: Two arms embowed, the dexter holding a rose gules, barbed, seeded, stalked and leaved proper, the sinister in armour proper holding a dagger argent hilted or Mantling: Gules and argent Mottoes: (above crest) E spinis (below shield) Merito

For James Bogle Delap, who m. Harriet, eldest dau. of Nathaniel Hillier, of Stoke Park, and d.s.p. 2 Nov. 1850, aged 71. (B.L.G. 5th ed.; M.I.)

2. All black background
On an ornamental lozenge suspended from a knot of blue ribbon
Arms: As 1.
Palm branches flanking lozenge
For Harriet, widow of James Bogle Delap. She d. 6 Jan. 1859, aged 75. (B.L.G. 5th ed.; M.I.)

3. All black background
Qly, 1st and 4th, Azure three roundels argent each charged with a squirrel sejant gules cracking a nut proper (Cresswell), 2nd and 3rd, Sable a chevron between three leopards' faces or (Wentworth)   To dexter of main shield, as main shield, impaling, Azure fretty argent (Cave) A.B1.   To sinister of main shield, as main shield, impaling, Or a water bouget sable, on a chief sable three bezants (Johnson) A.B1.
Crest: A squirrel sejant gules   Mantling: Gules and argent   Motto: In coelo quies
For John Wentworth Cresswell, who m. 1st, Penelope, dau. of Sir Roger Cave, and 2nd, Ann, dau. of William Johnson, and d. 11 Oct. 1759, aged 82. She d. 24 Jan. 1757. (M.I.)

4. All black background
Arms: Qly, as 3.
Crest and mantling: As 1.   Motto: In caelo quies   Cherubs' heads at sides of shield and winged skull in base
For William Wentworth Cresswell, who d. Apr. 1784. (M.I.)

MARLOW

1. All black background
Argent a cross between four roundels sable, at fess point the Badge of Ulster (Clayton), impaling, Or ermined sable a lion rampant sable (Kenrick)
Crest: A lion's gamb erased argent holding a roundel sable
Mantling: Gules and argent   Motto: In coelo quies
For Sir William Clayton, 1st Bt. (cr. 1732), who m. Martha (d. 14 Dec. 1739), dau. of John Kenrick, of Flore, Surrey, and d. 28 Dec. 1744. (B.P. 1949 ed.)

2. Dexter background black
Clayton, impaling, Argent a fess azure between three lions' heads erased proper langued azure (Fermor)   To dexter of main shield, Clayton, impaling, Azure a cross flory or (Warde) A.B1.

Buckinghamshire

To sinister of main shield, Clayton: In pretence, Azure a lion rampant argent between eight molets or (Lloyd) A.B1.
Crest: From a mural coronet gules a lion's gamb argent holding a roundel sable Mantling: Gules and argent Motto: Post funera virtus Skull below
For William Clayton, of Harleyford, who m. 1st, Mary, dau. of John Warde, of Squerries, Kent. She d. 2 Jan. 1760. He m. 2nd, 1761, Maria Eliza Catherina, elder dau. and co-heir of Rice Lloyd, of Alltycadno, Carms. She d. Dec. 1763. He m. 3rd, 1767, Louisa, dau. of Thomas, Earl of Pomfret, and d. 3 July 1783. She d. 30 June 1809.
(B.P. 1949 ed.)

3. Sinister background black
Qly, 1st and 4th, Clayton, 2nd and 3rd, Azure a lion rampant between eight molets or (Lloyd), over all the Badge of Ulster, impaling, Sable a chevron between three horses' heads erased argent (East)
Motto: My trust is in God
For Mary, only dau. of Sir William East, Bt., who m. 1785, Sir William Clayton, 4th Bt., and d. 9 Aug. 1833. (B.P. 1949 ed.)

4. All black background
Qly, as 3., with Badge of Ulster
Crests: Dexter, from a mural coronet gules a lion's gamb argent holding a roundel sable Sinister, A demi-lion rampant or Motto (over crests): Quid leone fortibus Mantling: Gules and argent
Motto: Virtus in actione consistit Supporters: Dexter, A leopard proper Sinister, A lion or semy of molets gules
Probably for Sir William Clayton, 4th Bt., who d. 26 Jan. 1834.
(B.P. 1949 ed.; M.I.)

5. Dexter background black
Two shields Dexter, within the Order of the Bath, Sable a lion passant argent between in chief two scaling ladders and in base a scimitar in bend argent hilted or (Morris) Sinister, within an ornamental wreath, as dexter, impaling, Qly, 1st and 4th, Sable a chevron between three stags' heads couped argent (Cocks), 2nd, Vert a fess dancetty ermine (Somers), 3rd, Or on a bend azure three pheons or (Thistlethwaite)
Crest: A demi-lion rampant argent crowned or holding a standard of St George Mantling: Gules and argent Motto: Resurgam
For Vice-Admiral Sir James Nicoll Morris, K.C.B., who m. 1802, Margaretta Sarah, dau. of Thomas Somers Cocks, and d. 15 Apr. 1830, aged 66. (M.I.)

6. All black background
Two shields Arms: As 5.
All on a white lozenge on a black background

Motto: Persevere   Cherub's head above and skull below
For Margaretta Sarah, widow of Vice-Admiral Sir James Nicoll Morris.
She d. 16 Jan. 1842. (M.I.)

7. **Dexter background black**
Gules an eagle displayed or (Ellison)   To dexter of main shield,
Ellison   In pretence: Argent on a chevron engrailed azure between
three greyhounds' heads erased sable ducally gorged or three molets of
six points or (Smith) A.B1.   To sinister of main shield, Ellison,
impaling, Argent a scythe, handle in bend sinister sable, in base a
fleur-de-lys sable (Sneyd) D.B1.
Crest: A griffin's head erased or   Mantling: Gules and argent
Motto: Extremum tibi semper adesse putes
For Thomas Ellison of the Inner Temple, who m. 1st, 1753, Elizabeth
Smith (d. 6 Feb. 1775), of St Saviour, co. Surrey, and 2nd, Sarah (d. 19
Sept. 1800), and d. 18 May 1800. (Foster's Marriage Licences; M.I.)

8. **Dexter background black**
Qly, 1st and 4th, Gules an eagle displayed or, on a canton argent a
fleur-de-lys sable (Ellison), 2nd, Azure on a bend argent between two
unicorns' heads erased argent armed or three fusils azure (Smith), 3rd,
Argent on a chevron azure between three greyhounds' heads erased
sable ducally gorged or three molets of six points or (Smith)
Crest, mantling and motto: As 7
Probably for George Ellison, who m. Mary, and d. 15 Dec. 1830. (M.I.)

9. **Dexter background black**
Azure a fess ermine between three eagles' heads erased or (? Spencer),
impaling, Gules three lozenge buckles argent pinned or over all a bend
argent (   )
Crest: An eagle rising argent armed gules between two stags' attires or
Mantling: Gules and argent   Motto: In coelo quies
Unidentified

10. **All black background**
On a lozenge   Argent gutty sable on a fess azure three towers or
(Higginson), impaling, Per pale gules and azure three eagles displayed or
(Coke)   Motto: Mors janua vitæ   Cherub's head above
For Elizabeth, dau. and heiress of Richard Coke of Melcombe Regis,
Dorset, who m. John Higginson, Citizen of London, and d.
(Autobiography of Gen. Sir George Higginson, Murray, 1916; M.I.)

11. **All black background**
Qly, 1st and 4th, Ermine on a fess sable three castles argent
(Higginson), 2nd and 3rd, Per pale gules and azure three eagles
displayed argent (Coke)

Crest: A turret or issuant therefrom a demi-griffin holding in its dexter claw a sword or   Mantling: Gules and argent   Motto: Beare and forbeare
For John, eldest son of John and Elizabeth, d. unm. 1780. (Sources, as 10.)

12. Dexter background black
Gules on a chevron between three cauldrons or three molets gules (Wethered)   In pretence: Ermine on a bend gules three eagles displayed or, in sinister chief a stag's head cabossed sable surmounted by a greyhound courant proper (Badger)
Crest: A goat's head erased proper   Mantling: Gules and argent
Motto: Virtute et labore
For Thomas Wethered, of Remnantz, nr Marlow, who m. 1788, Sarah, dau. and co-heir of Samuel Badger, of Fritwell and Weston, Oxon, and d. 7 Sept. 1849. (B.L.G. 1937 ed.; M.I.)

13. All black background
On a lozenge surmounted by a cherub's head   Arms: As 12.
Motto: As 12.
For Sarah, widow of Thomas Wethered. She d. 8 June 1856. (B.L.G. 1937 ed.; M.I.)

MEDMENHAM

1. Dexter background black
Qly, 1st and 4th, Argent a buglehorn sable stringed gules, on a chief azure three molets argent (Murray), 2nd and 3rd, Or on a bend azure a molet between two crescents or, on a bordure engrailed sable eight escallops or (Scott), impaling, Qly, 1st and 4th, Sable five roundels, two, two and one argent, on a chief argent a battleaxe fessways proper (Nixon), 2nd, Argent a chevron between three lions sejant sable langued gules (Lyons), 3rd, Or a lion rampant gules langued azure (? Colley)
Crests: Dexter, A demi-wildman affronté proper holding on his right shoulder a buglehorn sable   Sinister, A hart trippant proper attired argent   Mantling: Gules and argent   Mottoes: 1. (over dexter crest) Superna venabor   2. (over sinister crest) Free   3. (below shield) Resurgam
For Charles Scott-Murray, of Danesfield, Bucks, who m. 1815, Augusta Eliza, dau. of John Nixon, of Carrick, Westmeath, and d. 24 Apr. 1837. She d. 20 Jan. 1862. (B.L.G. 1937 ed.; M.I.)

MENTMORE

1. Sinister background black
Qly, 1st and 4th, Vert three primroses within a double tressure flory

counterflory or (Primrose), 2nd and 3rd, Argent a lion rampant doubletailed sable (Cressy)   In pretence: Qly, 1st, Or an eagle displayed sable langued gules, 2nd and 3rd, Azure, issuing from the dexter and sinister sides of the shield an arm embowed proper grasping five arrows points to the base argent, over all an escutcheon gules thereon a target point to the dexter proper, 4th, Or a lion rampant proper (Rothschild)   Countess's coronet   Crest: A demi-lion gules holding in the dexter paw a primrose as in the arms   Motto: Fide et fiducia   Supporters: Two lions or
For Hannah, only dau. and heiress of the Baron Meyer Amschel de Rothschild, of Mentmore, who m. Archibald, 5th Earl of Rosebery, K.G., and d. 19 Nov. 1890. He d. 21 May 1929. (B.P. 1949 ed.)

NEWTON BLOSSOMVILLE

1. **Dexter background black**
Argent on a bend engrailed gules three horseshoes argent (Farrer)   In pretence: Qly, 1st, per fess, in chief, Ermine a lion rampant or (Jones), in base, Azure three horses' heads erased two and one argent (Lloyd), 2nd, per fess, in chief, Azure three coronets in pale or (Beli Mawr), in base, Per bend sinister ermine and sable ermined argent a lion rampant or (Tudor Trevor), 3rd, Azure a lion rampant and a bordure argent (   ),4th, per fess, in chief, Argent a chevron sable, on a chief sable three birds argent (   ), in base, Gules a lion rampant guardant argent (   )
Crest: A horseshoe argent between two wings erect sable   Mantling: Gules and brown   Motto: Resurgam
For William Frederick Farrer, who m. Fanny Richarda, only child of Col. Love Parry Jones, and d. 1872. She d. 25 July 1879. (B.L.G. 1937 ed.)

PENN

1. **All black background**
Qly, 1st and 4th, Argent on a bend sable three martlets or collared gules (Curzon), 2nd and 3rd, Argent a molet sable (Assheton); in centre chief a crescent gules for difference   In pretence: Argent two lions passant guardant azure langued gules (Hanmer)   Also impaling two coats per fess, Azure a garb or (Grosvenor), Gules a lion rampant or (Meredith)   Viscount's coronet   Crest: A popinjay rising or collared gemel gules   Motto: Let Curzon holde what Curzon helde   Supporters: Two basilisks tails nowed or combed and wattled gules   All on a mantle gules and ermine
For Assheton, 1st Viscount Curzon, who m. 1st, 1756, Esther (d. 1764), only dau. and heir of William Hanmer of the Fenns, co. Flint,

Buckinghamshire 71

and 2nd, 1766, Dorothy (d. 1774), sister of Richard, 1st Earl Grosvenor, and 3rd, 1777, Anna Margaretta (d. 1804), dau. of Amos Meredith, and d. 21 Mar. 1820. (B.P. 1949 ed.)

2. Sinister background black
Two shields   Dexter, within Order of Hanover, Qly of six, 1st, Argent on a bend sable three popinjays or beaked, legged and collared gules (Curzon), 2nd, Argent on a fess sable three bezants (Penn), 3rd, Argent a molet pierced sable (Assheton), 4th, Hanmer, 5th, Argent a chevron between three plummets sable (Jennings), 6th, Or a fess between three wolves' heads erased sable (Howe)   Sinister, within wreath, Qly, as dexter (only parts of 5th and 6th qrs visible), impaling, Argent a chevron gules between three chapeaux gules and ermine (Brudenell) Countess's coronet   Supporters: Dexter, A basilisk tail nowed or combed and wattled gules   Sinister, A chough proper collared with a chain or   All on a mantle gules and ermine
For Harriet Georgiana Brudenell, who m. 1820, as his 1st wife, Richard William, 1st Earl Howe, and d. 25 Oct. 1836. (B.P. 1949 ed.)

3. Dexter background black
Qly of six, as 2., impaling, Vert on a fess or between three colts courant argent three roses gules barbed and seeded proper (Sturt)
Earl's coronet   Crests: Dexter, From a ducal coronet or a plume of five feathers azure   Sinister, A popinjay rising or beaked legged and collared gules   Motto: As 1.   Supporters: As 2.
For George Augustus, 2nd Earl Howe, who m. 1846, Harriet Mary, dau. of Henry C. Sturt, and d. 4 Feb. 1876. (B.P. 1949 ed.)

4. Dexter background black
Argent three towers sable (Haviland), impaling, Argent a fess and in chief three lozenges sable (Aston)
Motto: In coelo quies   Two cherubs' heads above shield, sprays of leaves flanking it, and winged skull below
For General William Haviland, of Penn, who m. 1st, 1748, Caroline (d. 1751), dau. of Col. Francis Lee, and 2nd, Salisbury (d. 1807), 2nd dau. of Thomas Aston, and d. 16 Sept. 1784. (B.L.G. 5th ed.; M.I.)

STOKE POGES

1. Sinister background black
Qly, 1st, Gules on a bend between six cross crosslets fitchy argent the Augmentation of Flodden (Howard), 2nd, Gules three lions passant guardant in pale or a label of three points argent (Brotherton), 3rd, Chequy or and azure (Warren), 4th, Gules a lion rampant argent (Mowbray), impaling, Sable a chevron between three leopards' faces or

(Wentworth)   Motto: Mors janua vitæ   Two cherubs' heads above shield
For Lucy, dau. of Thomas, 1st Earl of Strafford, who m. 1747, as his 1st wife, Field Marshal Sir George Howard, and d. 27 Apr. 1771.
(B.P. 1949 ed.; Annual Register, 178)

2. **Sinister background black**
Two shields   Dexter shield, within the Order of the Bath, Qly as 1., over all a crescent argent on a molet sable for difference   Sinister shield, within ornamental wreath, Qly as dexter, impaling, Per pale gules and azure on a chevron argent between three martlets or an eagle displayed sable (Beckford)
Crest: (above and between shields) On a chapeau gules and ermine a lion statant guardant tail extended or crowned azure and charged with a label of three points argent and a crescent argent on a molet sable for difference   Motto: (below dexter shield) Virtus mille scuta
Supporters: (one to each shield) Two lions rampant argent collared chequy or and azure, each charged with a crescent argent on a molet sable for difference   Star of Order below dexter shield, and flags and axes saltirewise behind both shields   To sinister of these two shields, a lozenge, ensigned with a countess's coronet, bearing the arms as dexter of 1., impaling, Beckford, but with a molet sable on dexter coat   Supporters: Two lions argent charged on the shoulder with a molet sable   All on a mantle gules and ermine   Cherub's head above
For Elizabeth, dau. of Peter Beckford of Jamaica, and widow of Thomas, 2nd Earl of Effingham, who m. 1771, as his 2nd wife, Field Marshal Sir George Howard, K.B., and d. 13 Oct. 1791.
(B.P. 1949 ed.; B.E.P.)

3. **All black background**
A shield and a lozenge   Dexter, shield, within Order of the Bath, Qly, as dexter of 2., but no crescent   Sinister, lozenge, ensigned with a countess's coronet, as dexter, impaling, Beckford
Crest: (above shield) On a chapeau gules and ermine a lion statant guardant tail extended or crowned gules   Motto: Virtus mille scuta
Supporters: (one to shield and one to lozenge) Two lions rampant argent collared counter-compony or and azure   All on a mantle gules and ermine
For Field Marshal Sir George Howard, K.B., who d. 16 July 1796.
(B.P. 1949 ed.; B.E.P.)

4. **Sinister background black**
Qly, 1st and 4th, Argent a stag's head cabossed between the attires a cross sable (Vyse), 2nd and 3rd, Howard with augmentation, charged on bend of 2nd quarter only with a crescent argent on a molet sable for difference, impaling, Or on a bend engrailed sable between two roundels gules three garbs or (Hesketh)

Motto: Virtus mille scuta   Cherub's head above
For Frances, 2nd dau. of Henry Hesketh, of Newtown, Cheshire, who m. 1810, Richard William Howard Howard-Vyse, and d. 14 Dec. 1841 (B.L.G. 1937 ed.; M.I.)

5. All black background
Arms: As 4., but with difference marks on both Howard coats
Crests: Dexter, From a mural coronet or a lion's head argent langued gules semy of roundels azure   Sinister, On a chapeau gules and ermine a lion statant guardant tail extended or crowned argent charged with a label of three points argent, also a crescent argent on a molet sable for difference   Mantling: Gules and argent   Motto: Virtus mille scuta
For Richard William Howard Howard-Vyse, who d. 8 June 1853, aged 67. (B.L.G. 1937 ed.; M.I.)

6. All black background
Qly, as 5., impaling, Argent on a pile vert three dexter hands apaumy argent (Jolliffe)
Crests: Dexter, From a mural coronet or a lion's head argent langued gules   Sinister, On a chapeau gules and ermine a lion statant guardant tail extended crowned or, charged as 5.   Mantling and motto: As 5.
For Richard Henry Howard-Vyse, of Stoke Place, who m. 1856, Julia Agnes, 3rd dau. of William, 1st Lord Hylton, and d. 12 June 1872, aged 59. She d. 29 Dec. 1862, aged 28. (B.L.G. 1937 ed.; M.I.)

7. Dexter background black
Argent on a fess sable three roundels argent (Penn), impaling, Argent a fess sable between three lions' heads erased gules (Fermor)
Crest: A demi-lion rampant argent collared sable the collar charged with three roundels argent   Mantling: Gules and argent   Motto: Dum clavum teneam
For Thomas Penn, who m. 1751, Juliana, 4th dau. of Thomas, !st Earl of Pomfret, and d. 21 Mar. 1775. (Burke's Commoners, Vol. 3; D.N.B.; Annual Register)

8. All black background
On a lozenge surmounted by a cherub's head
Penn, impaling, Argent a fess between three lions' heads erased sable (Fermor)
Motto: Resurgam
For Juliana, widow of Thomas Penn. She d. 20 Nov. 1801. (Source, as 7.)

9. All black background
Argent on a fess sable three roundels argent (Penn)
Crest: A demi-lion rampant argent collared sable, the collar charged

with three roundels argent   Above the crest on a scroll, Mercy and justice   Mantling: Gules and argent   Motto: Dum clavum teneam
Probably for John Penn, who d. unm. 21 June 1834. (Source, as 7.)

10. Dexter background black
Argent on a fess sable three roundels argent on a canton of Augmentation gules the crown of Charles II proper (Penn), impaling, Azure three bears' heads couped close argent muzzled gules (Forbes)   Crest: As 9. and on scroll above, Pennsylvania   Mantling: Gules and argent   Motto: Dum clavum rectum teneam
For Granville Penn, who m. 1791, Isabella, eldest dau. of General Gordon Forbes, and d. 28 Sept. 1844. (Source, as 7.)

11. All black background
On a lozenge surmounted by a cherub's head
Penn, as 10., impaling, Azure three bears' heads couped argent muzzled sable (Forbes)
Motto: In coelo quies
For Isabella, widow of Granville Penn. She d. 30 Sept. 1847. (Source, as 7.; M.I.)

12. Sinister background black (of sinister shield)
Two shields   Dexter, within the Order of the Bath, Argent a lion rampant sable armed and langued gules, on a chief gules two seaxes in saltire argent hilted or (Gomm)   Sinister, within a circlet, Gomm, impaling, Penn   Cherub's head above
For Sophia, dau. of Granville Penn, who m. Field Marshal Sir William Gomm, K.C.B., and d.s.p. 1 Mar. 1827, aged 33. (Source, as 7.; M.I.)

13. All black background
On a lozenge   Ermine a fleur-de-lys sable on a chief sable a molet or (Gayer)
Motto: Mors janua vitæ
Probably for Elizabeth, dau. of Robert Gayer. She was bur. 18 June 1714. (Par. Regs.)

14. Dexter background black
Qly, 1st and 4th, Azure on a bend engrailed or three martlets gules (Dawson), 2nd and 3rd, Azure three torches argent inflamed proper (Dawson)   In pretence: Argent a fess engrailed and in base a chevron sable (Freame)   Viscount's coronet   Crest: An estoile of six points or   Supporters: Dexter, A greyhound proper collared and chained sable   Sinister: An elk proper collared and chained sable   Motto: Toujours propice
For Thomas, 1st Viscount Cremorne, who m. 2nd, 1770, Philadelphia Hannah, only dau. of Thomas Freame, of Philadelphia, by Margaretta, dau. of William Penn, the founder of that city, and d. 1 Mar. 1813. (B.P. 1875 ed.)

Buckinghamshire

15. All black background
Qly, 1st and 4th, Qly ermine and azure a cross or (Osborne), 2nd and 3rd, Azure three cinquefoils between nine cross crosslets argent (Darcy), impaling, blank, filled with diapering
All on a doubleheaded eagle sable langued gules, with an imperial crown above Duke's coronet   Crests: 1. A heraldic tiger statant or maned and tufted sable   2. A dolphin naiant sable, with motto above, Franc ha leal eto ge   3. On a chapeau gules and ermine a bull statant sable, armed, unguled and tail tufted or   Supporters: Dexter, A griffin or ducally gorged azure   Sinister, A heraldic tiger argent ducally gorged azure   Motto: Pax in bello
For George Godolphin, 8th Duke of Leeds, who m. 1824, Harriette Emma Arundel Stewart, and d. 8 Aug. 1872. (B.P. 1949 ed.)

16. All black background
On a lozenge surmounted by a cherub's head
Ermine three lozenges conjoined in fess sable (Pigott), impaling, Or three piles issuant from the chief sable, a canton ermine (Wrottesley)
For Frances, dau. of the Very Rev. Sir Richard Wrottesley, 7th Bt., Dean of Worcester, who m. Admiral Hugh Pigot, brother of Lord Pigot, of Patshull, and d. 13 Apr. 1811. (B.P. 1939 ed.)

17. Dexter background black
Ermine on a cross sable four millrinds argent (Turner)   In pretence: Azure two bars argent, on a chief argent three roundels azure (Cramlington)
Crest: A lion statant guardant argent holding in its dexter paw a millrind sable   Mantling: Gules and argent   Motto: Spero
For Sir John Crichloe Turner, of Castle Carleton, Lincs, who m. 1779, Anne, only dau. and heiress of William Cramlington, of Newcastle-on-Tyne, and d. 7 Oct. 1813, aged 68. (B.L.G. 2nd ed.; M.I.)

18. All black background
On a lozenge surmounted by a skull
Dexter, per pale, Argent a lion rampant sable, the Badge of Ulster (Stapleton)   Gules three cinquefoils ermine (Hamilton)   In pretence (over impalement line) and impaling, Or on a bend between three molets sable three swans argent (Russell)
Motto: Mors janua vita   Cross bones on each side of lozenge
For Frances, dau. of Sir James Russell, who m. 1st, Sir William Stapleton, 3rd Bt., and 2nd, Colonel Walter Hamilton, Governor of the Leeward Islands, and d. 14 Jan. 1746. (Gents. Mag.; Complete Baronetage)

19. All black background
Per pale azure and sable a chevron engrailed ermine between three roundels argent (Woolhouse), impaling, Azure a fleur-de-lys argent (Digby)

Crest: An eagle's head erased sable ermined argent beaked gules ducally gorged or   Mantling: Gules and argent (ending in tassels)   A small hatchment, c. 2 ft x 2 ft
(This hatchment, in the Hastings Chapel, was formerly in the Hastings Almshouses. It is the earliest hatchment in the church, probably late 17th century)

20. Dexter background black
Ermine on a pile azure three eagles' heads argent (Halsey), impaling, Gules a chevron engrailed ermine between three eagles close argent (Child)
Crest: obliterated   Mantling: Gules and argent   Motto: Mors janua vitæ
For Edmund Halsey, M.P. for Southwark, who m. 1693, Anne, dau. and co-heir of John Child, and d.s.p.m. 19 Aug. 1729. (Romney Sedgwick, The House of Commons, 1715-1754)
(This hatchment was recorded in August, 1952, but is now missing)

21. All black background
Azure a paschal lamb proper (   ), impaling, Sable on a chevron between three molets of six points argent five lions' heads erased gules (   )
Crest: obliterated   Mantling: Gules and argent   Motto: Mors janua vitæ
Unidentified
(This hatchment was recorded in August, 1952, but is now missing)

STOWE

1. All black background
Two oval shields   Dexter, within the Garter, Qly of seven, 1st, Vert on a cross argent five roundels gules (Grenville), 2nd, Or an eagle displayed sable (Leofric), 3rd, Argent two bars sable each charged with three martlets or (Temple), 4th, Gules on a chevron or three lions rampant sable (Cobham), 5th, Ermine two bars gules (Nugent), 6th, Or a pile gules (Chandos), 7th, Argent on a cross sable a leopard's face or (Brydges)   Sinister, within an ornamental wreath, Qly as dexter, with in pretence: Qly of eight, 1st and 8th, Brydges, 2nd, Or a saltire and a chief gules, on a canton argent a lion rampant azure (Bruce), 3rd, qly i. and iv. Or on a pile gules between six fleurs-de-lys azure three lions of England (Seymour Augmentation), ii. and iii. Gules two wings conjoined in lure points downwards or (Seymour), 4th, Barry of six argent and azure in chief three roundels gules (Grey), 5th, Argent four bars gules a lion rampant or ducally crowned per pale argent and gules (Brandon), 6th and 7th, Qly France and England
Duke's coronet   Crest: A garb vert   Motto: Templa quam dilecta

Supporters: Dexter, A lion per fess embattled or and gules   Sinister, A horse argent semy of eaglets sable   All on a mantle gules and ermine   (N.B. 1st quarter of sinister shield is conjectural, being entirely covered by the dexter shield)
For Richard, 1st Duke of Buckingham and Chandos, K.G., who m. 1796, Anna Eliza (d. 15 May 1836), dau. and sole heir of James Brydges, 3rd and last Duke of Chandos, and d. 17 Jan. 1839. (B.P. 1875 ed.)
(The hatchment of his wife is at Avington, Hampshire)

WALTON

1. All black background
On a lozenge surmounted by a cherub's head
Azure on a chevron voided or between three doves proper three roundels argent (Pinfold)
Probably for Ann Pinfold, d. 5 Mar. 1806, aged 84. (M.I.)

WAVENDON

1. Dexter background black
Sable an eagle displayed with two heads argent, charged on the breast with an ermine spot, a bordure engrailed argent, in chief the Badge of Ulster (Hoare), impaling, Chequy argent and sable a fess gules (Acland)
Crest: An eagle's head erased argent   Mantling: Gules and argent
Motto: In coelo quies
For Sir Henry Hugh Hoare, 3rd Bt., who m. 1874, Maria Palmer (d. 31 Jan. 1845), dau. of Arthur Acland, and d. 17 Aug. 1841. (B.P. 1949 ed.)

2. Dexter background black
Qly, 1st and 4th, Hoare, without Badge of Ulster, 2nd and 3rd, Argent on a chevron engrailed gules three escallops or in chief a lion passant azure (Tully), impaling, Or on a cross flory gules a molet or (Ainslie)
Crest: An eagle's head erased argent charged with a crescent azure
Mantling: Gules and argent   Motto: In ardua
For Henry Charles Hoare, who m. 1821, Anne Penelope (d. 30 Mar. 1887), sister of Sir Robert Sharpe Ainslie, 1st Bt., and d. 15 Jan. 1852. (B.P. 1949 ed.)

3. Dexter background black
Qly, 1st and 4th, Hoare, without Badge of Ulster, 2nd, Or two bars sable each charged with three trefoils slipped argent, in chief a greyhound courant sable (Palmer), 3rd, Argent a fess embattled between three oxen sable (Oxenham), impaling, Per pale azure and gules three saltires couped argent (Lane)

Crest: An eagle's head erased argent charged with an ermine spot
Mantling: Sable and argent
For Henry Arthur Hoare, who m. 1859, Julia Lucy (d. 27 Aug. 1916), dau. of Thomas Veale Lane, and d. 6 Nov. 1873. (B.P. 1949 ed.)

NETHER WINCHENDON

1. All black background
Argent a chevron between three cocks gules armed, combed and jellopped or, on a chief sable three spearheads argent embrued proper, in fess point the Badge of Ulster, impaling, Or a lion rampant tail forked azure armed and langued gules between three roundels azure (Wankford)   Crest: A cock as in the arms
Mantling: Gules and argent   Motto: Non verbis sed factis
For the Rev. Sir Gilbert Williams, 5th Bt., who m. Dorothy, dau. of William Wankford, of Rickmansworth, and d. 9 Apr. 1768. (B.E.B.)

WINSLOW

1. Dexter background black
Qly, 1st and 4th, Argent fretty azure, each interlacing charged with a bezant, on a canton gules a leopard's head erased or gorged with a laurel branch proper (Lowndes), 2nd and 3rd, Or three bars sable within a bordure wavy gules (Selby), impaling, Argent two lions passant guardant azure (Hanmer)
Crests: Dexter, A leopard's head as in the arms   Sinister, A Saracen's head couped at the shoulders affronté proper, wreathed at the temples or and sable, belt and quiver or   Mantling: Azure and argent
Motto: Resurgam
For William Selby Lowndes, of Whaddon Hall, who m. 1806, Ann Eleanora Isabella (d. 30 Apr. 1852), dau. of the Rev. Graham Hanmer, and d. 18 May 1840. (B.L.G. 5th ed.)

WOOBURN

1. All black background
Argent three battering rams fesswise in pale or headed azure (Bertie)
Crest: A Saracen's head couped at the breast proper ducally crowned or
Mantling: Gules and argent   Motto: Virtus ariete fortior
For Peregrine Bertie, of Wooburn House, who d. 12 Oct. 1782.
(Gents. Mag.; V.C.H., Berkshire)

Buckinghamshire

WYCOMBE Abbey

1. Sinister background black
Ermine on a bend azure a magnetic needle pointing to the pole star or (Petty), impaling, Per bend embattled argent and gules (Boyle) Countess's coronet   Motto: Ut apes geometriam   Supporters: Dexter, A pegasus ermine winged and bridled or charged with a fleur-de-lys azure   Sinister, A lion rampant per pale embattled argent and gules
For Arabella, dau. of Charles, Viscount Dungarvan, who m. 1699, Henry Petty, 1st Earl of Shelburne, and d. Oct. 1740. (B.P. 1949 ed.)

2. All black background
Arms: As 1.
Earl's coronet   Crest: A beehive beset with bees diversely volant or Mantling: Gules and argent   Motto: Ut apes geometriam
Supporters: Dexter, A pegasus ermine winged and bridled or charged with a fleur-de-lys azure   Sinister, A lion per pale embattled argent and gules
For Henry Petty, 1st Earl of Shelburne, who d.s.p.s. 17 Apr. 1751. (B.P. 1949 ed.)

3. Sinister background black
Petty   In pretence: Qly or and gules a bend sable (Clavering) Viscountess's coronet   Motto: Je vise a ce seul astre   Supporters: Two pegasi ermine winged, unguled and bridled or, each charged with a fleur-de-lys azure
For Elizabeth, sister and co-heir of Sir James Clavering Bt. of Axwell, who m. James, Viscount Dunkerron, son of Henry Petty, 1st Earl of Shelburne, and d.s.p. 11 Aug. 1742. (B.P. 1875 ed.; Complete Peerage)

4. All black background
Arms: As 3., but with label for difference on Petty coat
Viscount's coronet   Crest: A hawk argent in the dexter claw a magnetic needle pointing to the polar star or   Mantling: Gules and argent   Motto and supporters: As 3.
For James, Viscount Dunkerron, who d. 17 Sept. 1750. (Sources, as 3.)

5. Sinister background black
Two oval shields   Dexter, Qly, 1st and 4th, Petty, 2nd and 3rd, Argent a saltire gules a chief ermine, in chief a crescent gules for difference (Fitzmaurice)   Sinister, Qly, 1st and 4th, Gules four lozenges in fess argent (Carteret), 2nd and 3rd, Gules three rests or (Granville)   Countess's coronet   Motto: Virtute non verbis Supporters: Dexter, A pegasus ermine winged and bridled or, charged with a fleur-de-lys azure   Sinister, A winged stag gules   Two cherubs' heads above

For Sophia, dau. of John, 1st Earl Granville, who m. as his 1st wife, William, later 1st Marquess of Lansdowne, and d. 5 Jan. 1771.
(B.P. 1949 ed.)

6. Sinister background black
Two oval shields   Dexter, within the Garter, Qly, 1st and 4th, Petty, 2nd and 3rd, Fitzmaurice   Sinister, within wreath, as dexter, impaling, Sable a saltire argent on a chief azure three fleurs-de-lys or (Fitzpatrick)   Marchioness's coronet   Motto: As 5.   Supporters: Dexter, A pegasus ermine winged or bridled gules   Sinister, A lion sable collared, chained and ducally crowned or   All on a mantle gules and ermine
For Louisa, dau. of John, 1st Earl of Upper Ossory, who m. as his 2nd wife, William, 1st Marquess of Lansdowne, and d. 7 Aug. 1789.
(B.P. 1949 ed.)

7. All black background
Arms (on two shields): As 6.
Marquess's coronet   Crest: A centaur proper   Motto, supporters, and mantle: As 6., but pegasus charged as 5.
For William, 1st Marquess of Lansdowne, K.G. who d. 7 May, 1805.
(B.P. 1949 ed.)

8. Dexter background black
Fitzmaurice, with crescent in dexter chief for difference   In pretence: Qly, 1st, Azure a ship sails furled within a royal tressure or (Orkney), 2nd and 3rd, qly. i. & iv. Gules three cinquefoils ermine (Hamilton), ii. & iii. Argent a ship sails furled sable (Arran), 4th, Argent a human heart gules imperially crowned or, on a chief azure three molets or (Douglas)   Shield in pretence ensigned with a countess's coronet
Crest: A centaur proper   Mantling: Gules and argent   Motto: Virtute non verbis
For the Hon. Thomas Fitzmaurice, son of John, 1st Earl of Shelburne, who m. Mary, Countess of Orkney, and d. 28 Oct. 1793.
(B.P. 1949 ed.)

9. Sinister background black
Or a chevron cotised between three demi-griffins the two in chief respectant sable (Smith), impaling, Qly, 1st and 4th, Argent a bear erect sable muzzled or (Barnard), 2nd and 3rd, Or three pallets gules on a saltire argent another couped azure (Boldero)
Baroness's coronet   Supporters: Two griffins sable beaked and winged or, the dexter charged with three fleurs-de-lys and the sinister with three trefoils or   All on a mantle gules and ermine
For Anne, dau. of Lewyns Boldero Barnard, of South Cave, Yorks, who m. 1780, as his 1st wife, Robert, 1st Lord Carrington, and d. 9 Feb. 1827. (B.P. 1949 ed.)

Buckinghamshire 81

10. Dexter background black (two dexter coats)
Qly, 1st and 4th, Argent a cross gules between four peacocks azure (Smith), 2nd, Argent on a bend sable three pairs of falchions in saltire argent hilted or (Carington), 3rd, Smith, as 9., impaling to dexter, Qly 1st and 4th, Barnard, 2nd and 3rd, Per pale or and azure a saltire counterchanged surmounted by another couped and counterchanged (Boldero), and impaling to sinister, Qly, 1st and 4th, Per chevron embattled or and azure three martlets counterchanged (Hudson), 2nd and 3rd, Argent a fret sable (   )
Baron's coronet   Crests: Dexter, A peacock's head erased azure ducally gorged or   Sinister, An elephant's head erased or eared gules charged with three fleurs-de-lys azure   Motto: In coelo quies
Supporters: Dexter, A griffin sable beaked or charged with three fleurs-de-lys or   Sinister, A lion gules gutty or
For Robert, 1st Lord Carrington, who m. 1st, Anne, dau. of Lewyns Boldero Barnard, and 2nd, 1836, Charlotte, 3rd dau. of John Hudson, and d. 18 Sept. 1838. She d. 22 Apr. 1849. (B.P. 1949 ed.)

11. Sinister background black
Azure two bars between six leopards' faces, three, two and one or (Shrimpton)   In pretence: Sable on a cross argent four millrinds sable (Turner)
Motto: Be ye also ready   Arms on a shield suspended by a lover's knot with cherubs' heads at top angles and winged skull in base
Unidentified

12. Dexter background black
Two oval shields   Dexter, as 11.   Sinister, Gules on a chevron argent a rose between two lions passant respectant gules (Hepburn)
Crest: A leopard passant proper   Mantling: Gules and argent
Motto: Be ye also ready   Winged skull in base
Unidentified

13. All black background
Qly, 1st and 4th, Argent two chevrons azure between three flames of fire proper (Welles), 2nd and 3rd, Chequy argent and vert a bend ermine (Sparkes)   In pretence: Qly, 1st and 4th, Sable three salmon naiant two and one argent (Welch), 2nd and 3rd, Azure a heraldic tyger statant or, on a chief or three crosses formy azure (Ewer)
Crest: A lion rampant sable langued gules   Mantling: Gules and argent   Motto: Regard the end
For Isabella, dau. of Thomas Welch of Gt. Hampden, who m. Samuel Welles, and d. 13 Mar. 1792. (Lipscombe; M.I.)

14. All black background
Welles   In pretence: Sable three salmon naiant in pale argent (Welch)

Crest, mantling and motto: As 13.   Mace and fasces in saltire at base, also winged skull
For Samuel Welles, who d. 15 Aug. 1807. (Sources, as 13.)

15. Sinister background black
Gules five pierced molets of six points in saltire or (three visible only) a canton ermine, an annulet argent charged with a fleur-de-lys in centre chief for difference (Westwood)   In pretence: Sable two chevrons argent between three flames of fire proper (Welles)
Motto: In coelo quies   Shield suspended from a lover's knot and flanked by two cherubs' heads at top angles
For Ann, eldest dau. of Samuel and Isabella Welles, who m. Thomas Westwood, Alderman of Wycombe, and d. 29 Jan. 1839. (Records of Buckinghamshire, Vol. 7; M.I.)

16. Sinister background black
Qly, 1st and 4th, qly. i. & iv. Azure three cinquefoils argent, ii. & iii. Gules three antique crowns or (Fraser), 2nd and 3rd, Azure a lion rampant argent within an orle of eight fleurs-de-lys or (   )   In pretence: Qly, 1st and 4th, qly i. & iv. Argent two chevrons azure between three flames of fire proper (Welles), ii. & iii. Chequy argent and vert a bend ermine (Sparkes), 2nd and 3rd, qly i. & iv. Vert three salmon naiant two and one argent (Welch), ii. & iii. Azure a lion statant or, on a chief or three crosses formy azure (Ewer)
On a shield surmounted by a cherub's head and surrounded by gilded foliage
For Charlotte, youngest dau of Samuel and Isabella Welles, who m. Henry Fraser, M.D. of Bath, and d. Mar. 1816. (Records of Buckinghamshire, Vol. 7.)

17. Dexter background black
Azure a cross botonny or (Ward), impaling, to dexter, Azure a pheon between three bucks trippant or (Green), and to sinister, Argent on a chevron engrailed between three cross crosslets fitchy sable two lions passant respectant argent (Barlow)
Crest: A wolf's head erased per fess or and sable langued gules
Mantling: Gules and argent   Motto: Jehovah jireh   Mace and fasces in saltire at base of shield
Probably for Charles Ward, Mayor of Wycombe, 1800–1801, and 1804–1805.

18. Dexter background black
Qly argent and gules in the second and third quarters a fret or (Dutton)
To dexter of main shield, Dutton, impaling, Sable a chevron ermine between three pelicans in their piety argent (Cullum) A.B1.   To

Buckinghamshire 83

sinister of main shield, Dutton, impaling, Gules a sword in bend argent hilted or (Gee) D.B1.
Crest: A plume of five feathers, argent, azure, or, sable, gules
Mantling: Gules and argent   Motto: Resurgam
Unidentified

19. All black background
Per pale ermine and azure a lion statant gules ducally crowned or within a bordure engrailed gules charged with fleurs-de-lys or (Bigg)
Crest: A leopard's face gules   Mantling: Gules and argent
Unidentified

20. All black background
Argent a chevron gules over all a bend azure (   )
No crest   Mantling: Gules and argent   Motto: Resurgam
Unidentified

WEST WYCOMBE

1. Dexter background black
Argent on a fess double cotised gules three griffins' heads erased or, in dexter chief the Badge of Ulster (Dashwood), impaling, Ermine a lion rampant proper collared and chained or in chief two eagles displayed gules (Broadhead)
Crest: A griffin's head erased per fess or ermined sable and gules
Mantling: Gules and argent
For Sir George Henry Dashwood, 5th Bt., who m. 1823, Elizabeth, dau. of Sir Theodore Henry Broadhead, and d. 4 Mar. 1862. (B.P. 1949 ed.)
(This hatchment was recorded from a photograph taken on Saturday 12 Apr. 1952, when the caves were re-opened for the first time after the war. Any tinctures given are therefore only presumed to be correct. The hatchment was hanging in a grotto over a pool, but it perished shortly afterwards)

OXFORDSHIRE

by

Peter Summers

Ashmolean Museum, Oxford: Reputed to be for John Tradescant, 1662
(*Photograph: Ashmolean Museum*)

INTRODUCTION

Eighteen of the ninety-seven hatchments recorded in the county are in the Colleges of the University. There is a particularly fine series at All Souls covering an almost unbroken span of 185 years from 1766 to 1951. The hatchment of Benedict Humphrey Sumner, who died in 1951, is the most recent example in the county, and there are eight others belonging to the present century. Two at New College are for well-known figures, Dr Spooner (famed for his Spoonerisms), who died in 1930, and H. A. L. Fisher, the historian, who died in 1940. Outside the Colleges, at the church of St Thomas the Martyr, is the hatchment of Charles Daniel, Provost of Worcester, who died in 1919; and in the Founder's Room of the Ashmolean, the most attractive little hatchment attributed to John Tradescant who died in 1662, whose collections were bequeathed to Elias Ashmole and eventually to the Museum. The best series is at Broughton, where there are ten hatchments of the Fiennes family, Lords Saye and Sele, the earliest being for Margaret Fiennes, who died in 1666, which is one of the earliest in the county. However, the earliest of all is the hatchment of Henry Jones at Chastleton House; he died in 1656. Another good series is in the Roman Catholic aisle of the parish church at Mapledurham; here are six hatchments of the Blount family, all recently restored.

The hatchment of Horace St Paul, Count of the Holy Roman Empire, may be seen in the bar of the Bay Tree at Burford. Horace's father was a brewer's son, and his mother a distiller's daughter, a splendid bottle-and-jug alliance. Where else could his hatchment have found a more suitable final resting place! Apart from Stonor Park where may be seen a Hudleston hatchment from Sawston Hall, Cambridgeshire, the only other hatchment alien to the county is in the possession of the editor, and he acquired it by purchase and serendipity. It hung originally at Buccleuch House,

Richmond, and it was recorded by him in 1953 at a private museum in Twickenham. He coveted it as the lady of the hatchment was an ancestress; it later appeared in a London sale together with a hatchment of a Duke of Northumberland, a marked catalogue being sent by an unknown friend. The two were bought by the editor (for £6!); the Northumberland hatchment has returned to its original home at Syon house, whilst the Buccleuch hatchment adds distinction to the hall of the editor's country cottage.

Peter Summers

BRIGHTWELL BALDWIN

1. **Dexter background black**
Qly of twelve, 1st, Azure a maunch ermine, over all a bend gules (Conyers, alias Norton), 2nd, Argent a chevron between three lozenge cushions sable (Norton), 3rd, Argent a bend engrailed between six martlets sable (Tempest), 4th, Ermine five fusils in fess gules (Hebden), 5th, Argent a chevron between three martlets gules (Waddington), 6th, Argent two bars and in chief three molets pierced gules (Washington), 7th, Gules a chevron between three bulls' heads cabossed argent (? Cowdell), 8th, Argent on a bend engrailed sable an escallop in chief argent (Radcliff), 9th, Sable a saltire argent (Rilleston), 10th, Argent a chevron between three maunches sable (Stafferton), 11th, Argent a fess between three escallops sable (   ), 12th, Sable a cross engrailed between four roundels argent each charged with a pheon sable (Fletcher), impaling, Qly of nine, 1st, Argent fretty azure the interlacings each charged with a bezant, on a canton gules a lion's head erased or (Lowndes) canton hidden by helm, 2nd, Gules a lion rampant argent a canton ermine (Scaringborne), 3rd, Lowndes, 4th, Argent two chevrons between three annulets sable (   ), 5th, Sable a handbow between two pheons argent (Cawarden), 6th, Gules three bendlets argent (Malveysin), 7th, Argent a chevron between three stags' heads cabossed gules attired or (Beckingham), 8th, Azure a chevron between three crosses formy or (Barclay), 9th Lowndes
Crest: A Moor's head couped affronté sable gorged with a chain or
Mantling: Gules and argent   Motto: Avi numerantur avorum
For the Rev. James Norton, who m. 1838, Isabella, only child of Thomas Lowndes, of Barrington Hall, Essex, and d. 31 Oct. 1853. She d. 26 Apr. 1877.   (B.P. 1949 ed.)

2. **Dexter background black**
Qly, 1st, qly i. & iv. Argent three cinquefoils sable a chief azure (Stone), ii. & iii. Argent fretty azure the interlacings each charged with a bezant, on a canton gules a lion's head erased or (Lowndes), 2nd, Sable on a bend argent three escallops gules (Layton), 3rd, Argent on a bend azure three wolves' heads erased argent (Lowe), 4th, Or two lions passant sable between three cross crosslets fitchy sable (Garth), impaling, Qly, 1st, Gules a chevron or between three crosses formy argent, on a canton ermine a stag's head erased facing sinister sable (Strickland), 2nd, Argent a cross between four nails gules (Pile), 3rd, Gules three fleurs-de-lys argent a chief vair (Palmes), 4th, Gules in chief

two helms argent and in base a garb or (Cholmeley)
Crests: Dexter, From a ducal coronet or a griffin's head ermine between two wings or   Sinister, A lion's head erased or gorged with a wreath of laurel proper   Mantling: Gules and argent   Motto: Mediocria firma   Winged skull below
For William Francis Lowndes-Stone, of Brightwell Park, J.P. & D.L., who m. 1811, Caroline, 2nd dau. of Sir William Strickland, 6th Bt., of Boynton, Yorks, and d. 1 Dec. 1858. She d. 11 Apr. 1867.
(B.L.G. 1937 ed.; M.I.)

BROUGHTON

1. Sinister background black
Azure three lions rampant or (Fiennes), impaling, Argent a saltire gules between four leaves vert, on a chief azure a lion's head erased between two battleaxes or (Burrell)
For Margaret, dau. and heiress of Andrewes Burrell, of the Isle of Ely, who m. as his 1st wife, the Hon. Richard Fiennes, 4th son of William, 1st Viscount Saye and Sele, and d. 17 Apr. 1666. (B.P. 1949 ed.; M.I.)

2. Sinister background black
Qly of six, 1st and 6th, Fiennes, 2nd, Qly argent and gules (Saye), 3rd, Argent two chevrons sable between three roses gules (Wykeham), 4th, Sable five molets in cross argent pierced gules (Perrott), 5th, Argent a chevron engrailed between three escallops sable (Trillow), impaling, Fiennes
Viscountess's coronet   Motto: Pour bein de siver   Supporters: Two wolf dogs argent gorged with spiked collars and chained or
For Mary, dau. of the Hon. Richard Fiennes, who m. 1670, as his 1st wife, William, 3rd Viscount Saye and Sele, and d. 23 Oct. 1676.
(B.P. 1949 ed.)

3. All black background
Qly of six, 1st, Fiennes, 2nd, Qly or and gules (Saye), 3rd, Wykeham, 4th, Perrott, 5th, Argent a chevron between three escallops sable (Trillow), 6th, Argent a bend wavy azure between two falcons close proper (Hobbs)
Viscount's coronet   Crest: An arm embowed vested sable the hand holding a mole spade proper   Mantling: Gules and ermine
Supporters: As 2.   Skull in base
For Lawrence, 5th Viscount Saye and Sele, who d. unm. 27 Dec. 1742.
(B.P. 1949 ed.)

4. All black background
Qly, 1st and 4th, Argent a chevron between three moles sable (Twisleton), 2nd and 3rd, Fiennes, impaling, Or two bars and in chief

Oxfordshire

three escallops azure (Clarke)
Crest: As 3.   Mantling: Gules and argent
For Fiennes Twisleton, de jure 11th Baron Saye and Sele, who m.
1692, Mary Clarke, and d. 4 Sept. 1730. (B.P. 1949 ed.)

5. All black background
On a lozenge   Qly, as 4., impaling, Or on a chevron gules between three griffins' heads erased azure two lions combatant argent (Gardner)
For Anne, dau. of William Gardner, of Little Bourton, who m. John Twisleton, de jure 12th Baron Saye and Sele, and d. 14 Jan. 1769. (B.P. 1949 ed.)

6. Dexter background black
Qly, 1st, Twisleton, 2nd, Fiennes with crescent for difference, 3rd, Saye, as 3., 4th, Wykeham, impaling, Qly, 1st and 4th, Argent a millrind sable (Turner), 2nd and 3rd, Azure a fess indented between three martlets or (Page)
Baron's coronet   Crest: As 3., but cuffed argent   Motto: Vidi vici   Supporters: As 2.
For Thomas Twisleton, 13th Baron Saye and Sele, who m. 1767, Elizabeth, dau. of Sir Edward Turner, 2nd Bt., and d. 1 July 1788. (B.P. 1949 ed.)

7. All black background
On a lozenge   Arms: As 6.
Baroness's coronet   Motto: Fortem posce animum   Supporters: As 2.   All on a mantle gules and ermine
For Elizabeth, widow of Thomas, 13th Baron Saye and Sele. She d. 1 Apr. 1816. (B.P. 1949 ed.)

8. Sinister background black
Qly of six, 1st, qly i. & iv. Fiennes, ii. Twisleton, iii. Argent on a chevron azure three garbs or, on a canton gules a fret argent in sinister chief an escallop sable (Eardley), 2nd, Saye, as 3., 3rd, Wykeham, 4th, Barry of ten argent and azure over all six escutcheons, three, two and one sable, each charged with a lion rampant argent (Cecil), 5th, Gules on a saltire argent an annulet sable (Nevill), 6th, Gules a fess between six cross crosslets or (Beauchamp)   In pretence: Eardley (no escallop)
Baroness's coronet   Supporters: As 2.
For Maria Marow, eldest dau. and co-heir of Sampson, Lord Eardley, who m. 1794, Gregory William, 14th Baron Saye and Sele, and d. 5 Sept. 1834. (B.P. 1949 ed.)

9. All black background
Arms: As 8., but no escallop on either Eardley coat
Baron's coronet   Crest: A wolf dog sejant argent collared and chained or   Motto: As 7.   Supporters: As 2.

For Gregory William, 14th Baron Saye and Sele, who d. 13 Nov. 1844. (B.P. 1949 ed.)

10. All black background
Qly of eight, 1st and 8th, qly i. & iv. Fiennes, ii. Twisleton, iii. Eardley, as 9., 2nd, Saye, 3rd, Wykeham, 4th, Cecil, 5th, Nevill, 6th, Beauchamp, 7th, Eardley
Baron's coronet Motto and supporters: As 9.
For William, 15th Baron Saye and Sele, who d. unm. 31 Mar. 1847. (B.P. 1949 ed.)

BURFORD

1. All black background
Qly, 1st and 4th, Sable a bend fusilly argent (Lenthall), 2nd and 3rd, Sable a chevron ermine between three leopards' faces argent (Hill)
Crest: A greyhound courant proper Mantling: Gules and argent
For William Lenthall of Burford, High Sheriff, Oxon, who d. unm. 22 Oct. 1781. (B.L.G. 1937 ed.; Gents. Mag. 492)

CHASTLETON House

1. All black background
Gules a lion rampant and a bordure indented or, a crescent on a molet for difference (Jones), impaling, Gules two chevrons argent a crescent for difference (Fettiplace)
Crest: A demi-lion rampant or, in its paws a molet gules Mantling: Gules and argent A small hatchment, c. 2 ft x 2 ft
For Henry Jones, of Chastleton, who m. 1609, Anne, dau. of Sir Edmund Fettiplace, and d. 10 Sept. 1656. (A History of Chastleton, M. Dickins)

CHISELHAMPTON

1. Dexter background black
Qly, 1st and 4th, Sable a chevron between three lions' heads erased argent a chief or (Peers), 2nd and 3rd, Or in chief three helms and in base a lion passant sable (Knapp), impaling, Qly, 1st and 4th, Sable a wolf rampant or (Lowth), 2nd and 3rd, Argent on a chevron sable between three eagles' heads erased azure three cinquefoils argent (Jackson)
Crest: A demi-griffin segreant wings addorsed argent Mantling: Gules and argent Motto: Resurgam

Oxfordshire 93

For Charles Peers, of Chiselhampton Lodge, who m. 1826, Mary, eldest dau. of the Rev. Robert Lowth, and d. 6th Feb. 1853. She d. 7 Feb. 1881. (B.L.G. 2nd ed.; Peers family)
(This hatchment was recorded in 1952, but is now missing)

CULHAM

1. Dexter background black
Or a lion rampant sable collared and chained or (Phillips), impaling, Argent a chevron sable ermined argent a canton gules (Shawe)
Crest: A demi-lion rampant sable collared and chained or   Mantling: Gules and argent   Motto: Resurgam
For John Phillips, of Culham House, who m. Frances Anne, dau. of William Cunliffe Shawe, and d. 2 July 1824. (M.I.)

2. Identical to 1.

DUCKLINGTON

1. Sinister background black
Gules a chevron or between three crosses formy argent, on a canton ermine a stag's head erased facing to the sinister sable (Strickland) In pretence: Qly, 1st and 4th, Sable a chevron between in chief two crescents and in base a trefoil slipped or (Western), 2nd, Per pale azure and gules a fleur-de-lys argent (ffolkes), 3rd, Ermine on a chief indented sable a fleur-de-lys between two ducal coronets argent (Taylor)   No frame
For Frances, dau. and co-heir of Maximilian Western, of Cokethorpe Park, who m. 1803, as his 1st wife, Walter Strickland, 3rd son of Sir George Strickland, 2nd Bt., and d. 23 Apr. 1836. (B.P. 1875 ed.)

2. Dexter five-eighths background black
Three coats per pale   1. *Strickland, with Western qly in pretence, as last   2. *Strickland, with a molet or for difference, impaling, Or a fess between three crescents gules (Boynton)
Crest: A turkey in pride proper   Mantling: Gules and ermine
Motto: Spe et fide   No frame   *Stag's head proper facing to dexter
For Walter Strickland, who m. 1837, Sarah (Bucktrout), widow of Sir Francis Boynton, Bt., and d. 26 Nov. 1839. She d. 11 Oct. 1877. (B.P. 1875 ed.)
(An unusual hatchment, with the husband's arms appearing twice, and the wife, presumably non-armigerous, using her first husband's arms)

HANWELL

1. Dexter background black
Argent on a chevron azure between three roses gules slipped and leaved proper three fleurs-de-lys or, the Badge of Ulster (Cope), impaling, Argent on a bend cotised gules three bezants (Bisshopp)
Crest: From a fleur-de-lys or a dragon's head gules   Mantling: Gules and argent   Motto: In coelo quies
For Sir Charles Cope, 2nd Bt., who m. 1767, Catherine, youngest dau. of Sir Cecil Bisshopp, Bt., and d. 14 June 1781. (B.E.B.)
(There is another hatchment for Sir Charles at Orton Longueville, Hunts)

HORLEY

1. All black background
Argent on a chevron gules between three lions' gambs sable armed gules three crescents or (Austin)   In pretence, and impaling, Per pale or and gules an eagle displayed sable (Stone)
Crest: Two lions gambs sable armed gules holding up a crescent or Mantling: Gules and argent
Unidentified
(This hatchment was recorded in bad condition in 1953, and has since disappeared)

2. All black background
Qly, 1st and 4th, Austin, 2nd and 3rd, Stone   In pretence: Stone
Crest and mantling: As 1
Perhaps for Edmund Stone Austin, d. 7 Aug. 1743, aged 46. (Inscr. on coffin)
(This hatchment was recorded in 1953, but has since disappeared)

KIDLINGTON

1. Sinister background black
Qly, 1st and 4th, qly i. and iv. Argent on a bend between two unicorns' heads erased azure three lozenges or ermined sable (Smith), ii. & iii., Azure on a mount vert a tower argent, on a chief or three storks' heads erased gules (Smith), 2nd and 3rd, Or six annulets sable a canton gules (Lowther)   In pretence: Per pale azure and gules a cross engrailed ermine (Barney)
Crest: An arm embowed or ermined sable the mailed hand proper holding a broken sword argent hilted or   Motto: Turris fortissima nomen domini
For Lydia, only child of Joshua Barney, of Walthamstow, who m. as his 1st wife, Joseph Smith, Ll.D. and d. 29 Apr. 1745. (Ox. Hist. Soc. XXIV, 1893)

Oxfordshire 95

2. Dexter background black
Qly, 1st, qly i. & iv. Azure on a mount vert a tower argent, on a chief or three cocks' heads erased gules (Smith), ii. & iii. Argent on a bend between two unicorns' heads erased azure three lozenges or ermined sable (Smith), 2nd, Qly France with a label of three points argent and England, a bordure compony argent and azure, a canton gules (Somerset), 3rd, Or six annulets sable (Lowther), 4th, Gules three lucies hauriant argent (Lucy) impaling, Sable a chevron ermine between three lions passant or (Bouchier)
Crest: As 1.   Mantling: Gules and argent   Motto: Ascendam
For Joseph Smith, who m. 2nd, Elizabeth Bouchier, and d. 10 Oct. 1776. (Source, as 1.)

3. All black background
On a lozenge   Arms: As 2.
Mantling: Gules and argent   No motto
For Elizabeth, widow of Joseph Smith. She d. 18 July 1777. (Source, as 1.)

KINGHAM

1. Dexter background black
Argent a fess engrailed between three cinquefoils and a bordure sable, a crescent for difference (Foley)   In pretence: Or a fess wavy between six billets sable (Dowdeswell)
Crest: A demi-lion rampant argent in its paws an escutcheon of the arms of Foley   Mantling: Gules and argent   Motto: Ut prosim
For the Very Rev. Robert Foley, D.D., Rector of Kingham, who m. Anne, dau. of the Rev. W. Dowdeswell, and d.s.p. 8 Jan. 1783. She d. 31 Oct. 1802. (B.P. 1939 ed.; M.I.)

KIRTLINGTON

1. All black background
Argent on a fess double cotised gules three griffins' heads erased or (Dashwood)   In pretence: Gules a saltire between four garbs or (Reade)
Crest: A griffin's head erased per fess or ermined sable and gules
Mantling: Gules and argent   Motto: Mors janua vitæ
For Robert Dashwood, who m. Dorothea, dau. and co-heir of Sir James Reade, Bt. of Brocket Hall, Herts, and d. 29 Sept. 1728. She d. 21 Apr. 1753. (B.P. 1949 ed.)

2. Dexter background black
Dashwood, with Badge of Ulster   In pretence: Gules an inescutcheon argent within an orle of eight molets or (Chamberlayne)

Crest and mantling: As 1.
For Sir Robert Dashwood, 1st Bt., who m. 1682, Penelope, dau. and co-heir of Sir Thomas Chamberlayne, Bt. of Wickham, Oxford, and d. 14 July 1734. (B.P. 1949 ed.)

3. **All black background**
On a lozenge   Arms: As 2.
For Penelope, widow of Sir Robert Dashwood, 1st Bt. She d. Feb. 1734/5. (B.P. 1949 ed.)

4. **Dexter background black**
Qly, 1st and 4th, Dashwood, with Badge of Ulster, 2nd, Chamberlayne, 3rd, Reade   In pretence: Qly argent and gules, in the second and third a fret or, over all on a bend sable three escallops argent (Spencer)
Crest and mantling: As 1.   Motto: In caelo quies
For Sir James Dashwood, 2nd Bt., who m. 1738/9, Elizabeth, dau. and co-heir of Edward Spencer, of Rendlesham, Suffolk, and d. 10 Nov. 1779. (B.P. 1949 ed.)

5. **All black background**
On a lozenge   Arms: As 4.
For Elizabeth, widow of Sir James Dashwood, 2nd Bt. She d. 19 Apr. 1798. (B.P. 1949 ed.; Complete Baronetage)

6. **Sinister background black**
Qly, 1st, Dashwood, 2nd, Chamberlayne, 3rd, Reade, 4th, Spencer, over all the Badge of Ulster, impaling, Argent a human heart gules crowned or, on a chief sable three escallops or (Graham)
Motto: Resurgam   Cherubs' heads at dexter and sinister angles of shield
For Mary Helen, dau. of John Graham, of the Supreme Court, Calcutta, who m. 1780, Sir Henry Watkin Dashwood, 3rd Bt., and d. 12 Oct. 1796. (Sources, as 5.)

7. **All black background**
Arms: As 6.
Crest: As 1.   Motto: Spero meliora
For Sir Henry Dashwood, 3rd Bt., who d. 10 June 1828. (B.P. 1949 ed.)

8. **Dexter background black**
Qly, as 6., with Badge of Ulster, impaling, Argent on a bend sable between two choughs proper three escallops argent (Rowley)
Crest and mantling: As 1.   Motto: Spero meliora
For Sir George Dashwood, 4th Bt., who m. 1815, Marianne Sarah, dau. of Sir William Rowley, 2nd Bt., and d. 22 Sept. 1861. She d. 24 Mar. 1877. (B.P. 1949 ed.)

MAPLEDURHAM

1. Dexter background black
Or three bars nebuly sable (Blount), impaling, Barry of six gules and argent on a chief or a lion passant azure (Englefield)
Crest: The sun in splendour proper   Mantling: Gules and argent, ending in tassels
For Lyster Blount, who m. 1663, Martha, dau. of Anthony Englefield, of Whiteknights, Berks, and d. 25 June 1710. She d. 31 Mar. 1743. (B.L.G. 1937 ed.)

2. All black background
Qly, 1st and 4th, Blount, as 1., 2nd, Argent two wolves passant sable, on a bordure gules ten saltires argent (Ayala), 3rd, Or a tower azure (Castile), impaling, Sable three escallops argent (Strickland)
Crest: The sun in splendour charged with an eye issuing tears proper, with motto 'Lux tua vita mea' above   Mantling: Gules and argent
Motto: Mors janua vitæ
For Michael Blount, who m. 1742, Mary Eugenia, dau. of Mannock Strickland, and d. 5 Feb. 1792. She d. 12 Dec. 1762. (B.L.G. 1937 ed.)

3. Dexter background black
Qly, 1st, Barry nebuly of eight or and sable (Blount), 2nd, Vair (Beauchamp), 3rd, Argent two wolves passant sable a bordure gules charged with ten cross crosslets or (Ayala), 4th, Or a tower azure (Castile)   In pretence: Qly, 1st and 4th, Gules a bend or between two escallops argent (Petre), 2nd and 3rd, Sable a chevron between three kites' heads erased or (Kite)
Crests: Dexter, as 2.   Sinister, On a ducal coronet or a wolf passant sable between two wings erect or   Mantling: Gules and argent
Mottoes: (above crests) Lux tua vita mea   (below shield) Resurgam
Frame decorated with skulls and crossbones
For Michael Blount, who m. 2nd, 1787, Catherine, dau. and heir of John Petre, of Belhouse, Essex, and d. 29 Oct. 1821. (B.L.G. 1937 ed.)

4. Dexter two-thirds background black
Barry nebuly of six or and sable (Blount), impaling, two coats per pale, 1st, Gules a bend or between two escallops argent (Petre), 2nd, Azure on a chevron between in chief two bees and in base a bull passant or three hawks bells sable (Wheble)
Crest: As 2., but no motto above   Mantling: Sable and argent, ending in tassels   Motto (below shield): Lux tua vita mea
For Michael Henry Mary Blount, who m. 1st, 1817, Elizabeth Anne Mary, 4th dau. of Robert Edward, 10th Lord Petre. She d. 4 Mar. 1848. He m. 2nd, Lucy Catherine, 4th dau. of James Wheble, of Bulmershe, Berkshire, and d. 3 Sept. 1874. (B.L.G. 1937 ed.)

5. All black background
Blount arms only, as 1.
Crest and mantling: As 2., but no motto
Probably for the Rev. Henry Tichborne Blount, who d. 29 May 1810.
(Commoners,Vol. 3)

6. Dexter background black
Qly, 1st and 4th, Blount, as 1., 2nd and 3rd, Vair a chief or (Tichborne)
Crest and mantling: As 2., but no motto above   Motto: Mors janua vitæ   Skull below
Probably for Joseph Blount, who m. Mary, dau. of Francis Canning, of Southcote, and d. 1 Jan. 1793. (Gents Mag. 91)
(All these hatchments have been recently restored: 1., 2., 4. and 5. by Messrs. Hazlitt, Gooden and Fox, 3. by Lt.-Col. R. L. V. ffrench Blake, and 6. by Mrs. Segal. They are in the Bardolf aisle and may be seen by appointment only)

MARSH BALDON

1. All black background
Qly, 1st and 4th, Sable a cross engrailed or, 2nd and 3rd, Gules a cross moline argent, all within a bordure compony argent and gules, in fess point the Badge of Ulster (Willoughby)
Crest: A Saracen's bust affronté couped at the shoulders proper ducally crowned or   Mantling: Sable and or   Motto: Verité sans peur
For Sir Henry Pollard Willoughby, 3rd Bt., of Baldon House, d. unm. 23 Mar. 1865. (B.P. 1875 ed.; M.I.)

NUNEHAM COURTENAY (old church)

1. Dexter background black
Gules two bars or (Harcourt), impaling, Qly, 1st and 4th, Barry of six azure and argent (Venables), 2nd and 3rd, Argent a fret sable (Vernon)
Earl's coronet   Crest: From a ducal coronet or a peacock proper
Mantle: Gules and ermine   Motto: Le bon temps viendra
Supporters: Two lions rampant or each gorged with a collar gemel or
Inscribed on frame: George Simon, 2nd Earl Harcourt, ob. April 1809.
For George Simon, 2nd Earl Harcourt, who m. 1765, his cousin, Elizabeth (d. 25 Jan. 1826), dau. of George, 1st Lord Vernon, and d.s.p. 20 Apr. 1809. (B.P. 1949 ed.)

2. Background black behind sinister half of sinister shield only
Two shields, the dexter slightly overlapping the sinister   Dexter, Gules two keys in saltire argent in chief an imperial crown or (See of

Oxfordshire 99

York), impaling, Qly, 1st and 4th, Harcourt, 2nd and 3rd, qly i. & iv.
Venables, ii. Argent a fret sable (Vernon), iii. Or on a fess azure three
garbs or (Vernon), the shield surmounted by a mitre issuing from a
ducal coronet or Sinister, as sinister of dexter shield, impaling,
Qly, 1st and 4th, Barry or eight argent and gules a cross moline sable
(Gower), 2nd and 3rd, Azure three laurel leaves erect or (Leveson),
the shield surmounted by a cherub's head
Inscribed on frame: Lady Anne Harcourt, ob. Nov. 1832.
For Anne, dau. of Granville, 1st Marquess of Stafford, K.G., who m.
1784, the Hon. and Rev. Edward Venables-Vernon (later Vernon-
Harcourt), and d. 16 Nov. 1832. (B.P. 1949 ed.)

3. Sinister background black
Arms: As dexter shield of 2., surmounted by a mitre issuing from a
ducal coronet or
Mantling: Gules and or Motto: Resurgam
Inscribed on frame, Edward, Archbishop of York, ob. Nov. 1847.
For the Rt. Hon. Most Rev. Edward Vernon-Harcourt, Archbishop of
York, who d. 5 Nov. 1847. (B.P. 1949 ed.)
(There is another hatchment for the Archbishop at Bishopthorpe, Yorks)

4. Dexter background black
Qly, 1st and 4th, Harcourt, 2nd and 3rd, qly. i. Argent a fret azure
(Vernon), ii. & iii. Venables, iv. Or on a fess azure three garbs or
(Vernon), impaling, Azure on a fess dancetty argent between three
griffins passant or three escallops gules (Holroyd)
Crest: From a ducal coronet or a peacock proper No helm or
mantling Motto: Le bon temps viendra
Frame inscribed: Edward William Harcourt ob. Dec. 1891.
For Edward William Harcourt, who m. 1849, Susan Harriet, dau. of
George, 2nd Earl of Sheffield, and d. 19 Dec. 1891. (B.P. 1949 ed.)

OXFORD All Souls College

1. Sinister background black
Or a chevron between three cinquefoils gules (All Souls), impaling,
Sable a serpent rising in pale proper, in chief a cinquefoil or between
two doves argent beaked and legged gules (Niblett), with, in pretence,
Argent a bend plain between two bendlets engrailed sable (Whitfield)
Crest: On a mount proper a lion couchant argent before a cross of
Calvary gules Mantling: Gules and argent
For Stephen Niblett, Warden 1726-1766, who m. Elizabeth, dau. and
heiress of Samuel Whitfield, of Winchcombe, and d. 1 June 1766.

2. Sinister background black
All Souls, impaling, Or an escallop in dexter chief sable between two
bendlets gules (Tracy)
Viscount's coronet Crest: On a chapeau gules and ermine an escallop

sable between two wings proper   Motto: Memoria in æterna
Supporters: Two eagles proper
For John, 7th Viscount Tracy, Warden 1766-1793, who d. 2 Feb.
1793.

3. **Sinister background black**
All Souls, impaling, Gules a fess wavy and in chief three piles wavy, a molet for difference or (Isham)
Crest: A demi-swan wings extended argent beaked or   Mantling: Gules and argent   Motto: Ostendo non ostento
For Edmund Isham, Warden 1793-1817, who d. 10 June 1817.

4. **Sinister one-third background black**
All Souls, impaling to dexter, the arms of the See of Oxford, and to sinister, Azure a stag's head cabossed argent (Legge)
On a rococo shield surmounted by an esquire's helm ensigned with a mitre
Mantling: Gules and argent   Motto: Gaudet tentamine virtus
For the Rt. Rev. the Hon. Edward Legge, Bishop of Oxford, Warden 1817-1827, who d. 27 Jan. 1827.

5. **Sinister background black**
All Souls, impaling, Argent a scythe enclosing a fleur-de-lys, a crescent for difference sable (Sneyd)
Crest: A lion passant guardant sable   Mantling: Gules and argent
Motto: Resurgam
For Lewis Sneyd, Warden 1827-1858, who d. 21 Feb. 1858.

6. **Sinister background black**
All Souls, impaling, Qly per fess indented or and gules (Leighton)
Motto: Dread shame
For Francis Knyvett Leighton, Warden 1858-1881, who d. 13 Oct. 1881.

7. **Sinister background black**
All Souls, impaling, Qly, 1st, Argent three bends engrailed a crescent gules for difference (Anson), 2nd, Ermine three cats-a-mountain passant guardant in pale azure (Adams), 3rd, Azure three salmon naiant in pale per pale or and argent (Sambrooke), 4th, Sable a bend between three spearheads argent (Carrier), the Badge of Ulster over line of impalement
Crest: From a ducal coronet or a spearhead erect proper   Mantling: Gules and argent   Motto: Nil desperandum
For Sir William Reynell Anson, 3rd Bt., Warden 1881-1914, who d. 4 June 1914.

Oxfordshire

8. Sinister background black
All Souls, impaling, Gules a griffin segreant or within an orle of eight roses argent barbed and seeded proper (Thesiger)
Viscount's coronet   Crest: A cornucopia fesswise the horn or the fruit proper, thereon a dove holding in its beak a sprig of laurel proper
Mantling: Gules and argent   Motto: Spes et fortuna   Supporters: Two griffins or wings vair
For Frederick, 1st Viscount Chelmsford, Warden 1932-1933, who d. 1 Apr. 1933.

9. Sinister background black
All Souls, impaling, Ermine two chevrons gules (Sumner)
For Benedict Humphrey Sumner, Warden 1945-1951, who d. 25 Apr. 1951.

Lincoln College

1. Sinister background black
Lincoln College, impaling, Barry of six or and sable an escutcheon argent, on a chief or two pallets between two gyrons sable (Mortimer)
Crest: A stag's head argent semy-de-lys sable   Mantling: Gules and argent   Motto: In coelo quies
For Charles Mortimer, Rector 1781-1784, who d. 26 Aug. 1784.

2. Sinister background black
Lincoln College, impaling, Argent a cross formy azure (Tatham)
Crest: A lion passant guardant proper   Mantling: Gules and or
Motto: Resurgam
For Edward Tatham, Rector 1792-1834, who d. 24 Apr. 1834.

3. Sinister background black
Lincoln College, impaling, Sable fretty argent on a chief gules three hawks' bells or (Radford)
Crest: A hawk close proper belled or   Mantling: Gules and argent
Motto: Resurgam
For John Radford, Rector 1834-1851, who d. 21 Oct. 1851.

4. Sinister background black
Lincoln College, impaling, Or on a fess dancetty sable three estoiles argent, on a canton sable a sun in splendour or (Thompson)
Crest: A cubit arm vested gules cuffed argent the hand proper holding three ears of wheat or   Mantling: Gules and argent
Motto: Resurgam
For James Thompson, Rector 1851-1860, who d. 26 Dec. 1860.

5. Sinister background black
Lincoln College, impaling, two coats per pale, 1st, Argent three griffins'
heads erased azure langued gules a bordure engrailed azure (Pattison),
2nd, Ermine on a fess vert three eagles displayed or (Winn)
Crest: A greyhound's head erased proper   Mantling: Gules and
argent   Motto: Non sibi sed patriæ
For Mark Pattison, Rector 1861-1884, who d. 30 July 1884.

(There are a number of minor variations in the College arms, especially
in the Fleming coat: all five hatchments have the names of the Rectors,
and their dates in office, painted on the frames)

New College

1. All black background
Sable a chevron between three bees volant argent (Sewell), impaling,
Argent two chevrons sable between three roses gules barbed and seeded
proper (New College)
Crest: A dexter arm in armour sable cuffed and elbowed or, the hand
holding a staff in pale supporting a skip proper
An inaccurately marshalled hatchment
For James Edwards Sewell, Warden 1860-1903, who d. 29 Jan. 1903.

2. Sinister background black
New College, impaling, Azure on a bend argent a boar's head couped
gules distilling blood proper (Spooner)
Crest: A boar's head couped or armed argent langued gules transfixed
through the neck with a spear in fess argent embrued gules
Mantling: to dexter, Sable and argent, and to sinister, Azure and argent
Motto: Optima loquere pulcherrima fac   On a wood panel
For Dr William Archibald Spooner, Warden 1903-1924, who d.
29 Aug. 1930.

3. Sinister background black
New College, impaling, Sable on a mount vert two stags combatant
argent langued gules, attired, unguled, ducally gorged and lined or
(Fisher)
Crest: A demi-stag couped ermine, attired, unguled and gorged with a
coronet and corded or   Mantling: Sable and argent   Insignia of
Order of Merit pendent below   On a wood panel
For the Rt. Hon. Albert Laurence Fisher, Warden 1925-1940, who
d. 18 Apr. 1940.

Queen's College

1. All black background
Argent a lion rampant between two dexter hands in chief gules,

Oxfordshire

debruised by a fess or charged with two lions rampant supporting a sinister hand gules (Neale)   On an oval shield
Mantling: Gules and argent   Motto: Loyal au mort
A small hatchment, c. 2 ft x 2 ft
For John Alexander Neale, a benefactor, who d. 1 Dec. 1930.

Ashmolean Museum

1. All brown background
Or on a bend wavy sable three fleurs-de-lys or, in chief a crescent for difference (for Tradescant)
Crest: On a chapeau gules and ermine a fleur-de-lys or between two wings sable   Mantling: Gules and argent
A small hatchment c. 1½ ft x 1½ ft including frame, which is decorated with cherubs' heads in relief at the corners and formal decorations between
Believed to be for John Tradescant, who d. 22 Apr. 1662. (D.N.B.; tomb in Lambeth churchyard).

St Thomas the Martyr

1. Sinister background black
Or two chevrons between six martlets three, two and one gules (Worcester College), impaling, Argent a pale fusilly sable (Daniel)
Crest: A cross crosslet fitchy argent between two wings or
Mantling: Gules and argent   Motto: Cruce itur ad astra
For Charles Henry Olive Daniel, Provost of Worcester, 1903-1919, who d. 6 Sept. 1919.

ROUSHAM

1. Dexter background black
Argent a bend between three escallops sable (Cottrell)   In pretence: Qly of six, 1st and 6th, Argent three roses gules barbed and seeded proper, on a chief gules three roses argent barbed and seeded proper (Adelmare, alias Caesar), 2nd, Argent two bars sable, on a chief sable three pelicans vulning themselves argent (Cesaryno), 3rd, Gules three crescents argent (Perient), 4th, Or three lozenges conjoined in fess vert over all a bendlet gules (Angel), 5th, Azure on a cross argent a roundel gules (Bonfoy)
Crest: A talbot's head erased sable langued gules collared and chained or the collar charged with three escallops sable   Mantling: Gules and argent   Motto: Multis ille bonis flebilis occidit
For Sir Charles Cottrell-Dormer, who m. Jane, dau. and co-heir of Charles Adelmare Caesar, and d. 29 Dec. 1779. (B.L.G. 1937 ed.; M.I.)

2. Sinister background black
Cottrell   In pretence: Sable three horses' heads erased argent (Heylin)
Motto: In celo quies   Cherub's head above and palm branches at sides
For Elizabeth Heylin, 1st wife of Sir Clement Cottrell-Dormer.   She d. 28 Apr. 1800. (Sources, as 1.)

3. Dexter background black
Cottrell   In pretence: Heylin   Also impaling, Vert a chevron between three bucks trippant or (Robinson)
Crest and mantling: As 1.   Motto: Nec temere nec timide
For Sir Clement Cottrell-Dormer, who m. 1st, 1783, Elizabeth Heylin, and 2nd, Margaret Robinson, and d. 27 Oct. 1808. (Sources, as 1.)

4. All black background
On a lozenge surmounted by an escallop and surrounded by gilt scrollwork   Cottrell, impaling, Robinson
For Margaret, widow of Sir Clement Cottrell-Dormer. She d. 10 Aug. 1834. (Sources, as 1.)

5. Dexter background black
Qly, 1st and 4th, Azure ten billets or from a chief or issuant a demi-lion rampant sable (Dormer), 2nd and 3rd, Argent a bend between three escallops sable (Cottrell), impaling, Gules a chevron or between three crosses formy argent, on a canton ermine a stag's head erased sable (Strickland)
Crests: Dexter, A fox passant proper   Sinister, A talbot's head erased sable collared and chained argent the collar charged with three escallops sable   Mantling and motto: As 3.
For Charles Cottrell-Dormer, J.P., D.L., High Sheriff 1828, who m. 1826, Frances Elizabeth, eldest dau. of Walter Strickland, of Cokethorpe Park, Oxon, and d. 2 Dec. 1874. (B.L.G. 18th ed.)

6. Dexter background black
Qly, as 5., impaling, Sable a cross moline argent (Upton)
Crest: A fox statant proper   Mantling and motto: As 3.
For Clement Upton-Cottrell—Dormer, J.P., D.L., who m. 1858, Florence Anne, 2nd dau. of Thomas Upton, of Ingmire Hall, Westmorland, and d. 29 Dec. 1880. She d. 17 Jan. 1907. (B.L.G. 1937 ed.)

SANDFORD ST MARTIN

1. Sinister background black
Or on a bend azure an estoile of eight points between two crescents or (Scott), impaling, Per chevron engrailed gules and argent three talbots' heads erased counterchanged (Duncombe)

Countess's coronet   Motto: Amo   Supporters: Two females, each vested azure and wearing on her head a plume of three ostrich feathers argent
For Anne, dau. and heir of William Duncombe, of Battlesden, Beds, who m. as his 1st wife, Henry, 1st Earl of Deloraine, and d. 22 Oct. 1720. (B.E.P.)

2. All black background
Or on a bend azure an estoile of six points between two crescents or, a crescent for difference (Scott) Shield surrounded by Order of the Bath, and surmounted by an earl's coronet   To dexter of main shield, Scott, impaling, Per chevron engrailed gules and argent three talbots' heads erased counterchanged (Duncombe), the shield surmounted by an earl's coronet A.B1.   To sinister of main shield, Scott, impaling, Qly, 1st, Gules on a bend between six cross crosslets fitchy argent, the Augmentation of Flodden (Howard), 2nd, Gules three lions passant guardant in pale or a label of three points argent (Brotherton), 3rd, Chequy or and azure (Warren), 4th, Gules a lion rampant or (Fitzalan), the shield surmounted by an earl's coronet D.B1.
Crest: A stag trippant or   Mantling: Gules and argent   Motto: Amo
Supporters: As 1.
For Henry, 1st Earl of Deloraine, who m. 1st, Anne, dau. and heir of William Duncombe, of Battlesden, Beds, and 2nd, Mary, dau. of Philip, son of Thomas, 1st Earl of Berkshire, and d. 25 Dec. 1730. (B.E.P.)

3. All black background
Qly or and sable a cross flory counterchanged, in the first quarter a ducal coronet gules (Taylor)
Crest: A greyhound's head quarterly argent and sable ducally gorged or   Mantling: Gules and argent   Motto: Mors janua vitæ
Unidentified

4. All black background
Arms: As 3.
Crest: A greyhound's head quarterly argent and sable collared or the collar charged with a ducal coronet gules   Mantling: Gules and argent
Unidentified

5. All black background
Qly, 1st and 4th, Gules a chevron argent between three doves proper (Sayer), 2nd and 3rd, Azure a lion rampant or (Hughes), a molet for difference in centre chief of shield
No crest   Motto: Vive memor lethi   Flags in saltire behind shield
Skull in base
For Vice-Admiral James Sayer, who d. 29 Oct. 1776, aged 56. (M.I.)

SOMERTON

1. Dexter background black
Argent a fess sable between three lions' heads erased gules (Fermor), impaling, Sable a fess between three sheldrakes argent (Sheldon)
Crest: From a ducal coronet or a cock's head gules beaked combed and wattled or   Mantling: Gules and argent
For Henry Fermor, who m. 1736, Frances, dau. of Edward Sheldon of Beoley, and d. 17 Jan. 1746/7. She d. 20 Mar. 1790. (Baker's Northants, i, 599; Complete Baronetage)

2. Sinister background black
Fermor, impaling, Argent two bars and in chief three escallops azure (Errington)
Motto: Resurgam   Two cherubs' heads above shield
For Frances, eldest dau. of John Errington, of Beaufront, Northumberland, who m. 1766, William Fermor of Tusmore, and d. 24 June 1787. (Sources, as 1.)

3. All black background
Arms: As 2.
Crest: defaced   Mantling: Gules and argent   Motto: Horæ sempre
For William Fermor, of Tusmore, who d. 1 July 1806. (Sources, as 1.)

SPELSBURY

1. Dexter background black
Qly, 1st, Argent a lion passant between three crescents gules (Dillon), 2nd, Argent a fess between three crescents sable (Lee), 3rd, Gules a chevron or, on a canton or a molet sable (for Pope), 4th, qly. i. & iv. qly England and France, ii. Scotland, iii. Ireland, with harp imperially crowned, over all a baton sinister gules, sable and gules (for Fitzroy)
On a cartouche surrounded by the collar of a Knight of St Patrick, with Badge pendent below
Viscount's coronet   No crest   Mantling: Gules and ermine
Motto: Virtus post funera vivit   No supporters   Cherub's head to dexter and sinister
For Charles, 12th Viscount Dillon, K.P., who m. 1st, 1776, Henrietta Maria (d. 1 Sept. 1782), only dau. of Constantine, 1st Baron Mulgrave, and 2nd, 1787, Marie Rogier, of Malines, Belgium, and d. 9 Nov. 1813. She d. 28 Aug. 1833. (B.P. 1949 ed.)

2. Dexter background black
Qly, 1st, Dillon, 2nd, Lee, 3rd, Qly France and England (for Fitzroy), 4th, Or two chevrons gules, on a canton gules a molet or (Pope), impaling, Qly, 1st and 4th, Argent an eagle with two heads displayed sable (Browne), 2nd and 3rd, Sable three lions passant in bend between four bendlets argent (Browne)

Oxfordshire

Viscount's coronet   Crest: A demi-lion gules holding between the
paws an estoile of six points argent   Motto: Dum spiro spero
Supporters: Two angels proper vested argent, the dexter with a sash
over the shoulder azure, each holding in the exterior hand a palm
branch proper   All on a mantle gules and ermine
Printed on back of canvas: Prepared by Roberson and Miller, 51 Long
Acre, London   R & M 576
For Henry Augustus, 13th Viscount Dillon, who m. 1817, Henrietta
(d. 18 Mar. 1862), eldest dau. of Dominick Geoffrey Browne, M.P., and
d. 24 July 1832. (B.P. 1949 ed.)
(These hatchments were restored in 1979 by Lt.-Col. R. L. V. ffrench
Blake)

SWALCLIFFE

1. **Dexter background black**
Argent two chevrons sable between three roses gules (Wykeham),
impaling, Gules on a bend between two demi-lions argent three
fleurs-de-lys azure (Hughes)
Crest: A bull's head erased sable charged with two chevrons argent
Mantling: Gules and argent   Motto: Resurgam   Cherubs' heads
above
For William Richard Wykeham, of Swalcliffe, who m. 2nd, Mary, dau.
of Thomas Hughes, and d. 1 July 1800. (B.L.G. 1937 ed.: Lipscombe)

SWERFORD

1. **All black background**
Argent on a chevron gules three lions passant guardant or (Bolton)
The circular shield surrounded with the Order of Hanover, with the
cross of the Order pendent below
Crest: A stag's head couped in its mouth an arrow proper   Mantling:
Gules and argent   Motto: Vi et virtute   Flags and cannons in saltire
behind shield
For Lieut.-General Sir Robert Bolton, G.C.H., who d. 15 Mar. 1836.
(M.I.)

GREAT TEW

1. **Dexter background black**
Qly, 1st and 4th, qly i. & iv. Or an escallop in dexter chief sable
between two bendlets gules (Tracy), ii. & iii., Azure a cross crosslet
fitchy or (Ethelred), 2nd, Argent a cross cotised of demi-fleurs-de-lys
between four molets sable (Atkyns), 3rd, Sable a bend or ermined sable
cotised flory or (Keck), impaling, Gules a fess chequy argent and
azure between three lozenges argent (Lindsay)

Crest: On a chapeau gules and ermine an escallop sable between two wings or   Mantling: Gules and argent   Motto: In coelo quies
Two cherubs' heads above and skull below
For John Tracy Atkyns, cursitor baron of the Exchequer, who m. Katharine Lindsay, and d. 23 July 1773. (D.N.B.)

2. All black background
Qly, 1st and 4th, Sable a bend ermine cotised flory or (Keck), 2nd and 3rd, Argent a fess nebuly sable between three lozenges gules in chief a lion passant azure (Thorne)   In pretence: Sable a chevron between three towers triple-towered argent (Dunch)
Crest: From a mural coronet gules a maiden's head affronté, couped at the shoulders proper vested ermine crined and wreathed or
Mantling: Gules and argent   Motto: Mors janua vitæ
For Francis Keck, son of Sir Anthony Keck, by Mary, dau. of Francis Thorn, who m. Mary, dau. of Major Dunch, of Pusey, Berkshire, and d. 29 Sept. 1728. (Notes and Queries, 27/11/48)

3. Dexter background black
Qly, 1st and 4th, Keck as 2., 2nd, Thorne, 3rd, Dunch   In pretence, and impaling, Azure a lion rampant argent between eight fleurs-de-lys or (Poole)
Crest and mantling: As 2.   Motto: Fugaces labuntur anni
For John Keck, son of Francis Keck, who m. Mary Poole, and d. 13 Aug. 1729. (Source, as 2.)

4. Sinister background black
Qly, 1st and 4th, Tracy, 2nd and 3rd, Keck as 2., over all a molet on a crescent for difference, impaling, Qly, 1st and 4th, qly i. & iv., Gules three cinquefoils argent (Hamilton), ii. & iii. Argent a lymphad sable (Arran), 2nd and 3rd, Argent a human heart gules imperially crowned proper, on a chief azure three molets argent (Douglas)
Crest and mantling: As 1.
For Susan, dau. of James, 4th Duke of Hamilton, who m. Anthony Tracy Keck, son of John Tracy of Stanway, by Ann Atkyns, and d. 3 June 1755. (Source, as 2.)

5. All black background
Qly, 1st and 4th, qly i. & iv. Tracy, ii. & iii. Azure a cross potent fitchy or (Ethelred), 2nd and 3rd, Keck as 2., over all a molet on a crescent for difference, impaling, Hamilton qly as 4.
Crest and mantling: As 1.
For Anthony Tracy Keck, who d. 29 May 1767. (Source, as 2.)

6. Dexter background black
Qly, 1st, Tracy, with a martlet on a crescent for difference, 2nd and 3rd, Keck as 1., 4th, Azure a cross crosslet fitchy or (Ethelred)

In pretence: Qly, 1st and 4th, Vert a fess between three roses argent barbed sable (Dodwell), 2nd and 3rd, Barry of six argent and gules a canton gules (Fuller)
Crest and mantling: As 1.   Motto: Pareo non servio
For Thomas Tracy Keck, brother of Anthony, who m. Mary, dau. and heir of Sir W. Dodwell, by Mary, dau. of Francis Fuller, and d. 24 June 1770. (Source, as 1.)

7. Dexter background black
Or on a chief indented azure three escallops argent (Stratton), impaling, Gules a chevron between three swans argent (Light)
Crest: A falcon rising or   Mantling: Gules and argent
For George Stratton, who m. Hester Eleanor Light, and d. 20 Mar. 1800, aged 65. (Sources, as 1.; M.I.)

8. All black background
Qly, 1st, Azure on a bend or cotised argent between two fleurs-de-lys or an anchor between two leopards' faces sable (Boulton), 2nd, Or a heraldic tyger passant sable (Dyott), 3rd, Vert on a chevron between three stags trippant or three trefoils slipped sable (Robinson), 4th, Argent ten roundels four, three, two and one gules, a label of three points azure (Babington), impaling, Azure a chevron between three whelkshells or (Wilkinson)
Crest: A hind's head erased at the neck gules, the head per pale azure and or, in the mouth a bird bolt or feathered argent   Mantling: Vert and or   Motto: Faire mon devoir
For Matthew Robinson Boulton, of Great Tew, who m. 1817, Mary Anne, dau. of William Wilkinson, of Plas Grono, co. Denbigh, and d. 18 May 1842. She d. 1829. (Sources, as 7.; B.L.G. 1937 ed.)

WHEATFIELD

1. Dexter background black
Qly, 1st and 4th, Qly argent and gules in the second and third a fret or, over all on a bend sable three escallops argent (Spencer), 2nd and 3rd, Sable a lion rampant argent, on a canton argent a cross gules (Churchill), impaling, Qly, 1st and 4th, Argent a bear sejant sable muzzled and collared or (Bernard), 2nd, Azure a griffin segreant within an orle of eight leopards' faces jessant-de-lys or (Morland), 3rd, Vert a saltire engrailed argent (Tyringham)
Crests: Dexter, From a ducal coronet or a demi-griffin argent beaked and collared sable the collar charged with three escallops argent   Sinister, A lion couchant guardant argent in its dexter paw a banner gules charged with a sinister hand couped argent   Mantling: Gules and argent   Motto: In coelo quies

For the Rev. Frederick Charles Spencer, Rector of Wheatfield, who m. 1823, Mary Ann, dau. of Sir Scrope Bernard Morland, Bt., and d. 2 Oct. 1831, aged 35. She d. 21 Jan. 1882. (B.P. 1868 ed.; M.I.)

WOOD EATON

1. Sinister background black
Ermine on a cross gules five escallops or (Weyland)   In pretence: Gules a fess between two chevrons argent (Nourse)
Motto: Resurgam   Cherub's head above
For Elizabeth Johanna, dau. and co-heir of John Nourse, of Wood Eaton, who m. 1772, John Weyland, of Woodrising, Norfolk, and Wood Eaton, and d. 8 Feb. 1822. (B.L.G. 1937 ed.)

2. All black background
Arms: As 1.
Crest: A lion rampant sable langued gules   Mantling: Gules and argent   Motto: Resurgam
For John Weyland, who d. 24 July 1825, aged 81. (B.L.G. 1937 ed.)
(There is also a hatchment for John Weyland in the parish church at Woodrising, Norfolk)

3. Sinister background black
Qly, 1st and 4th, Weyland, 2nd and 3rd, Nourse, impaling, Azure three boars' heads erased or within a bordure countercompony or and azure (Gordon)
Mantling: Gules and argent   Motto: Resurgam   Cherub's head above
For Charlotte, dau. of Charles Gordon of Cluny, and widow of Sir John Lowther Johnstone, Bt., who m. Richard Weyland, High Sheriff and M.P. for Oxon, and d. 1 Dec. 1845. (B.L.G. 1937 ed.)

4. All black background
Arms: As 3., but boars' heads erased close
Crests: Dexter, A lion rampant sable   Sinister, A cubit arm vested azure cuffed argent the hand proper grasping a snake vert
Mantling: Gules and argent   Motto: Resurgam
For Richard Weyland, who d. Oct. 1864. (B.L.G. 1937 ed.)
(There is also a hatchment for Richard Weyland in the parish church at Woodrising, Norfolk)

5. All black background
Nourse arms only
Crest: As sinister of 4.   Mantling: Gules and argent   Motto: In caelo quies
Possibly for John Nourse, d. 1 Apr. 1708.

Oxfordshire

BURFORD (The Bay Tree)

1. Dexter background black
Qly, 1st and 4th, Argent a lion rampant gules crowned or (St Paul),
2nd and 3rd, Argent an eagle displayed sable (St Paul), impaling, Sable
a chevron or between three wolves' heads erased argent langued gules
(Weston)   Above the shield a coronet of a Count of the Holy Roman
Empire   Motto: Esse quam videri   Supporters: Two lions
reguardant argent langued gules each supporting a spear, from the
dexter a flag argent charged with a lion rampant gules crowned or, from
the sinister a flag argent charged with an eagle displayed sable
For Horace St Paul, son of Robert St Paul, of Doddington,
Northumberland, cr. a Count of the Holy Roman Empire, 1759,
m. 1774, Anne, only dau. of Henry Weston, of West Horsley Place,
Surrey, and d. 16 Apr. 1812. She d. 5 Aug. 1838. (Foster's Peerage
1880 ed.; Ancestor, Vol. 7; pp. 17-21)

The following hatchments are privately owned and no longer in the
parishes to which they originally belonged.

STONOR Park

1. All black background
Qly of six, 1st, Gules fretty argent (Huddleston), 2nd, England within a
bordure argent (Holland, Earl of Kent), 3rd, Gules a saltire argent a
label compony argent and azure, a crescent for difference (Nevill),
4th, Argent three fusils conjoined in fess gules (Montagu), 5th, Or an
eagle displayed vert (Monthermer), 6th, Or a lion rampant gules
(Charlton)
Crest: Two arms embowed vested argent holding a scalp proper
Mantling: Gules and argent   Motto: Soli Deo honor et gloria
Unidentified
(This hatchment came from Sawston Hall, Cambridgeshire)

NORTH STOKE

1. All black background
On a lozenge   Qly, 1st, qly i. & iv. Qly France and England,
ii. Scotland, iii. Ireland, over all a baton sinister argent, 2nd, qly i. & iv.
Argent three fusils conjoined in fess gules within a bordure sable
(Montagu) ii. & iii. Or an eagle displayed vert (Monthermer), 3rd,
qly i. & iv. Argent a human heart gules crowned with an imperial
crown or, on a chief azure three molets argent (Douglas), ii. & iii.
Azure a bend between six cross crosslets fitchy or (Mar), all within

a bordure or charged with a double tressure flory counterflory gules, 4th, Argent on a bend azure an estoile of six points between two crescents or (Scott)   In pretence: Qly, 1st and 4th, Montagu, 2nd and 3rd, Monthermer   Duchess's coronet   Supporters: Dexter, A unicorn argent, maned and unguled or, ducally gorged and chained or   Sinister, A griffin or langued gules, wings elevated and addorsed sable   Arms and supporters on a mantle gules and ermine
For Elizabeth, dau. of George, Duke of Montagu, who m. 1767, Henry, 3rd Duke of Buccleuch, K.G., and d. 21 Nov. 1827. (B.P. 1949 ed.)
(This hatchment, which came originally from Buccleuch House, Richmond, is now in the possession of Mr Peter Summers, Day's Cottage, North Stoke. There is an identical hatchment at Boughton House, Northamptonshire.)

WILTSHIRE

by

Peter Summers

Boyton: For H.R.H. Prince Leopold, Duke of Albany, 1884
(*Photograph by Mr. S. Slater*)

INTRODUCTION

Wiltshire is a county rich in hatchments, not only in numbers (nearly 150 have been recorded, 25 of them in Salisbury), but in their wide range of interest. Six have disappeared since the Survey began in 1952.

The earliest hatchments are at Preshute, one 1648 and the other, which has not been identified, probably of about the same date. A third, and particularly fine, example (of 1667) was stolen in 1970. At the other end of the scale Kilmington has four hatchments of which the earliest is 1894, the other three being 1906, 1911 and 1947, all for members of the Paynter family. Another recent hatchment, which cannot now be traced, was seen by the editor hanging over the main entrance of Wardour Castle on the death of Lord Arundell in 1947.

Few royal hatchments are known but at Boyton may be seen Prince Leopold's: it is of normal size and shape, though on a wood panel instead of the more usual canvas. And at Codford St Peter is a small rectangular hatchment, with identical arms, painted on silk and elaborately framed.

The many-quartered hatchment of Anne Mynors-Baskerville at Winterborne Bassett is of interest in that it is identical to one at St Weonards, Herefordshire; her husband's hatchment is at Clyro in Radnorshire.

In the Blackmore Museum in Salisbury there are two armorials, of the Merchant Taylors Company and the Bakers Company. The former is of diamond shape, but only about two feet square, and the latter is rectangular and also small. Both were probably used at the funerals of members of the Companies.

There is a Royal Arms of Queen Anne at Box. As it is dated 1714 this may have been erected as a hatchment on her death; this possibility is strengthened by the tradition that she was a friend of Dame Rachel Speke, of Hazelbury Manor in the parish. It is also of diamond shape but this is not an uncommon feature of Royal Arms in the West Country.

There are several rectangular panels and memorial boards in the county. A few of these which bear no inscription have been included, and the others will be dealt with in a subsequent volume. Two which are very close to classification as hatchments are at Everleigh and Salisbury Cathedral, both being for John Barnston, Prebendary of Salisbury, who died in 1645. Another very similar in style is for a member of the Snell family at Yatton Keynell.

Peter Summers

ALDBOURNE

1. All black background
Argent a chevron between three garbs gules (   )
Crest: A hind statant or   Mantling: Gules and argent   Motto: Deo pro nobis
Unidentified

AMESBURY

1. Dexter background black
Lozengy or and azure on a pale gules three estoiles or, in chief the Badge of Ulster (Antrobus), impaling, Qly, 1st and 4th, Gules a fess chequy argent and azure (Lindsay), 2nd and 3rd, Or a lion rampant gules over all a ribbon sable (Abernethy)
Crest: Issuing out of rays proper a unicorn's head couped argent armed and maned or, gorged with a wreath of laurel vert   Mantling: Azure and or   Motto: Dei memor gratus amici   Supporters: Two horses argent
For Sir Edmund Antrobus, 2nd Bt., who m. 1817, Anne, only dau. of the Hon. Hugh Lindsay, and d. 4 May 1870. (B.P. 1949 ed.)

AVEBURY

1. All black background
Qly, 1st and 4th, Or on a chevron gules between three trefoils slipped sable a boar's head between two molets or (Williamson), 2nd, Sable three lozenges argent on a chief or three fleurs-de-lys sable (Pedley), 3rd, Argent on a fess azure three molets argent in chief a boar's head erased sable (?Hutcheson)
The shield surrounded with the Order of the Bath
Crest: From a mural coronet gules charged with two molets argent a wyvern's head sable breathing fire proper   Mantling: Gules and argent
Motto: Resurgam   Supporters: Two lions rampant gules each murally collared or with the inscription 'St Domingue' thereon
For Lieut.-General Sir Adam Williamson, K.C.B., Governor of Jamaica and San Domingo, who died from the effects of a fall at Avebury House, 21 Oct. 1798. (D.N.B.)

GREAT BEDWYN

1. All black background
Two shields   Dexter, within the Order of the Thistle, Qly, 1st and 4th, Argent a saltire and a chief gules, on a canton argent a lion rampant azure (Bruce), 2nd and 3rd, Argent a chevron gules between three morions azure (Brudenell)   Sinister, within an ornamental wreath, Qly as dexter, impaling, to the dexter, Sable a doubleheaded eagle displayed within a bordure engrailed argent (Hoare), and to the sinister, Argent a fess between three pheons sable (Rawdon)
Earl's coronet   Crest: A lion statant tail extended azure
Mantling: Gules and ermine   Motto: Fuimus   Supporters: Two wild men wreathed about the loins and temples with laurel proper
For Thomas, 1st Earl of Ailesbury, K.T., who m. 1st, 1761, Susanna, dau. of Henry Hoare, of Stourhead, and 2nd, 1788, Anne, 3rd dau. of John, 1st Earl of Moira, and d. 19 Apr. 1814. (B.P. 1949 ed.)

2. Dexter background black
Two shields   Dexter, as 1.   Sinister, within an ornamental wreath, Qly as dexter, impaling to the dexter, only ermine visible but presumably Hill, and to the sinister, Argent a fret sable (Tollemache)
Marquess's coronet   Crests: Dexter, as 1.   Sinister, A seahorse argent   Supporters: As 1., but each holding in their exterior hands a staff with a banner bearing the arms of Bruce
For Charles, 2nd Earl and 1st Marquess of Ailesbury, K.T., who m. 1st, 1793, Henrietta Maria, dau. of Noel, 1st Baron Berwick, and 2nd, 1833, Maria Elizabeth, dau. of the Hon. Charles Tollemache, and d. 4 Jan. 1856. (B.P. 1949 ed.)

3. Sinister background black
Qly of nine, 1st, Or a saltire and a chief gules, on a canton argent a lion rampant azure, a label of three points sable for difference (Bruce), 2nd, Or on a pile gules between six fleurs-de-lys azure three lions passant guardant or (Seymour Augmentation), 3rd, Gules two wings conjoined in lure points downwards or (Seymour), 4th, Barry of six argent and azure in chief three roundels gules, a label of three points ermine (Grey), 5th, Vairy or and gules (Ferrers), 6th, Barry of eight argent and gules over all a lion rampant or ducally crowned argent (Brandon), 7th, Argent a fess and in chief three roundels gules (Devereux), 8th, Argent a cross engrailed gules between four water bougets sable (Bourchier), 9th, Qly France and England a bordure argent (Plantagenet), impaling, Per bend embattled argent and gules (Boyle)
Viscountess's coronet   Motto: Fuimus   Supporters: Dexter, A wild man wreathed about the loins and temples with laurel proper   Sinister, A lion rampant per pale embattled argent and gules
For Juliana, dau. of Charles, 3rd Earl of Cork and 2nd Earl of

Burlington, who m. 1719, as his 2nd wife, Charles, Viscount Bruce, later 4th Earl of Elgin and 3rd Earl of Ailesbury, and d.s.p. 26 Mar. 1739. (B.P. 1949 ed.)
(This hatchment, for many years at Bloxham Lodge, is now in the possession of Lord Ailesbury)

BERWICK ST JOHN

1. Sinister background black
Ermine on a chevron engrailed gules an escallop or between two escallops argent (Grove), impaling, Qly or and gules on a bend sable three crosses formy fitchy or (Hanham)
For Eleanor, dau. of Sir William Hanham, of Dean's Court, Dorset, who m. as his 1st wife, John Grove, of Ferne, and d. 27 Mar. 1754.
(B.P. 1949 ed.; M.I.)

2. Dexter background black
Ermine on a chevron engrailed gules three escallops or (Grove), impaling, Sable a lion rampant between eight cross crosslets argent (Long)   Crest: A talbot statant sable collared argent   Mantling: Gules and argent   Motto: Ny dessux ny dessoux
For John Grove, of Ferne, who m. 2nd, Philippa, dau. of Walter Long, of Close Gate, Sarum, and d. 28 Feb. 1769. (Sources, as 1.)

3. All black background
On a lozenge surmounted by a cherub's head
Grove, as 1., impaling, Sable crusilly a lion rampant argent (Long)
For Philippa, widow of John Grove, of Ferne, d. 26 June 1805.
(Sources, as 1.)

4. All black background
Grove, as 1., impaling, Azure a lion rampant or holding in the dexter paw a dagger argent, on each of two flaunches or an anchor proper (Pilfold)
Crest: A talbot passant sable collared engrailed argent
Mantling: Gules and argent
For Thomas Grove, of Ferne, who m. 1781, Charlotte, dau. of Charles Pilfold, of Effingham, Surrey, and d. 22 Apr. 1847. She d. 12 Apr. 1828. (Sources, as 1.)

5. Dexter background black
Grove, as 1., impaling, Qly, 1st and 4th, Azure a bend engrailed between two cinquefoils argent, a canton gyronny of eight or and sable (Fraser), 2nd and 3rd, Argent three antique crowns gules (Fraser)
Crest and mantling: As 4.   Motto: As 2.
For John Grove, of Ferne, who m. 1818, Jean Helen, dau. of Sir William Fraser, Bt., and d. 14 Apr. 1858. (Sources, as 1.)

6. Sinister background black
Grove, as 2., in dexter chief the Badge of Ulster, impaling, Per pale gules and azure three lions passant guardant per pale argent and or the second charged with a portcullis sable (O'Grady)
Crest, mantling and motto: As 5.
For Katherine Grace, 2nd dau. of the Hon. Waller O'Grady, who m. 1847, Sir Thomas Fraser Grove, 1st Bt., and d. 8 June 1879.
(Sources, as 1.)

BOWDEN HILL, nr Chippenham

1. All black background
Argent a savage's head couped affronté distilling drops of blood proper, about the temples a wreath of holly vert, within an orle of eight martlets sable (Gladstone), impaling, Argent three bats' wings erect couped sable, on a chief gules a lion passant guardant argent (Bateson)
Crest: Issuant from a wreath of holly a demi-griffin proper supporting between the claws a sword argent hilted or the blade enfiled with a wreath of oak proper   No mantling   Motto: Fide et virtute
For John Neilson Gladstone, of Bowden Park, who m. 1839, Elizabeth Honoria, dau. of Sir Robert Bateson, Bt., and d. 7 Feb. 1863.
(B.P. 1949 ed.)

BOX

1. All black background
Qly, 1st and 4th, Or on a bend engrailed gules three cross crosslets fitchy argent (Richmond), 2nd and 3rd, Per fess gules and argent a cross flory between four molets counterchanged (Webb)
Crest: A tower argent   Mantling: Gules and argent   Motto: Mors janua vitæ
Unidentified
(The dexter half of the shield has been almost completely obscured with black paint)

BOYTON

1. Dexter background black
Two oval shields, the dexter overlapping the sinister   Dexter, within the Garter, Qly, 1st and 4th, England, 2nd, Scotland, 3rd, Ireland, in chief a label of three points argent charged on the centre with a cross gules and on the outer points with a heart gules   In pretence: Saxony   Sinister, within a wreath of oakleaves, Qly of nine, 1st and 9th, Argent a cross moline gules (Pyrmont, 1st covered by dexter shield), 2nd and

Wiltshire

8th, Argent three escutcheons gules (Rappolstein), 3rd and 7th, Argent three ravens' heads couped proper ducally crowned or (Hoheneck), 4th and 6th, Argent billetty azure a lion rampant gules ducally crowned or (Geroldseck), 5th, hidden by escutcheon: over all an escutcheon, Or a molet of eight points sable (Waldeck) Royal duke's crown above Motto: Dieu et mon droit   Supporters: Dexter, A lion rampant guardant crowned or charged with a label as in the arms   Sinister, A unicorn argent armed, maned, tufted and unguled or, gorged with a crown with chain reflexed over the back or, charged with a label as in the arms   On a wood panel, with wide black frame
For H.R.H. Prince Leopold, K.G., Duke of Albany, who m. 1882, H.S.H. Princess Helen, dau. of H.S.H. George Victor, Prince of Waldeck and Pyrmont, and d. 28 Mar. 1884. (B.P. 1949 ed.)
(*see also* Codford St Peter)

BRADFORD-ON-AVON

1. All black background
Qly, 1st, Azure a lion rampant between eight quatrefoils argent a chief or (for Shrapnel), 2nd and 3rd, qly i. & iv. Argent a bend or (for Scrope), ii. Sable a saltire or (   ), iii. Sable a saltire or over all two bars gules (   ), 4th, Gules a fess engrailed ermine between three griffins' heads erased proper (   )   In pretence: Argent a bomb fired proper
Crest: From a ducal coronet or five ostrich feathers argent
Mantling: Or   Motto: Ratio ultima regum   A cherub's head on either side of shield and below
For Lieut.-General Henry Shrapnel, Colonel Commandant, 6th Battalion of Artillery, inventor of the shrapnel shell, who d. 13 Mar. 1842, aged 80. (M.I.; D.N.B.)

BRINKWORTH

1. Sinister background black
Argent on a chevron engrailed sable between three estoiles gules three bucks' heads cabossed or (Ayliffe), impaling, Argent on a chief gules two molets argent, in fess point a crescent sable for difference (St John)
A rectangular panel, c. 2 ft x 1½ ft
For Anne, dau. of Sir John St John of Lydiard Tregoze, who m. Sir George Ayliffe, and d.
(The 'hatchment' of Sir George Ayliffe is at Lydiard Tregoze)

BROAD HINTON

1. Dexter background black
Qly of twelve, 1st, Paly of six or and azure, on a chief gules three crosses formy or, at honour point the Badge of Ulster (Meux), 2nd,

Ermine four barrulets gules (Huntercombe), 3rd, Ermine a lion passant gules (Drewe), 4th, Gules on a chevron between three cinquefoils or five molets pierced azure (Kingston), 5th, Azure three cinquefoils and in chief a boar passant or charged with a cross formy gules (Massingberd), 6th, Qly or and argent four lions rampant sable, over all a plain cross couped gules charged with seven escallops or (Massingberd), 7th, Ermine a fess gules (Button), 8th, Argent a bend between six cross crosslets fitchy azure (Woodthorpe), 9th, Argent a chevron between three cross crosslets sable within a bordure sable charged with ten roundels argent (Mablethorpe), 10th, Sable three helms within a bordure engrailed argent (Halliday), 11th, Azure a lion rampant within an orle of ten cross crosslets argent (Braytoft), 12th, Vert a lion rampant argent (Arden), impaling, Qly, 1st and 4th, Or a saltire and a chief gules, on a canton argent a lion rampant azure (Bruce), 2nd and 3rd, Argent a chevron gules between three morions proper (Brudenell) Crest: Two wings conjoined in lure points downwards argent joined with a ring and cord or   Mantling: Gules and argent   Motto: Ut sursum desuper
For Sir Henry Meux, 2nd Bt., who m. 1856, Louisa Caroline, dau. of the Rt. Hon. Lord Ernest Bruce, and d. 1 Jan. 1883. (B.P. 1939 ed.)

2. Sinister background black

Qly argent and sable on a bend gules three molets or (Calley), impaling, Sable a bend ermine cotised flory counterflory or (Keck)
No crest, mantling or motto
For Elizabeth Anne, dau. of Anthony James Keck, who m. Thomas Calley, and d. 16 Apr. 1832. (B.L.G. 2nd ed.)

3. Dexter background black

Qly, 1st and 4th, Gules a bezant between three demi-lions rampant argent, on a canton or a cross engrailed gules (Bennet), 2nd, Ermine a bend fusilly gules (Pye), 3rd, Gules a cross engrailed argent, on an inescutcheon argent a dexter arm in armour proper emerging from the sinister, the hand holding a staff with a pennon gules, within an orle of eight molets sable (Legh)   In pretence: Bennet
Crests: Dexter, A lion's head erased gules charged on the neck with a bezant   Sinister, A cross crosslet fitchy gules between two wings expanded argent   Mantling: Gules and argent   Motto: In cruce glorior
For William Bathurst Pye Bennet of Salthrop, who m. Elizabeth, 2nd dau. and co-heiresss of Peter Legh, of Lyme, by Martha, only child of Thomas Bennet, and d.
(V.C.H. Wilts, xi, 241; Earwaker, East Cheshire, ii.; B.L.G.)

4. All black background

On a lozenge surmounted by a cherub's head
Qly, 1st and 4th, Bennet, 2nd, Pye, 3rd, Gules a cross engrailed argent,

on an inescutcheon argent a dexter arm embowed in armour proper emerging from the sinister, holding a staff with a pennon divided fesswise gules, argent and azure (Legh)   In pretence: Bennet
Skull below
For Elizabeth, widow of William Bathurst Pye Bennet. She d.
(Sources, as 3.)

BULFORD

1. Dexter background black
Qly, 1st and 4th, Or a chevron between three apples gules (Southby), 2nd and 3rd, Per fess argent and azure three chaplets counterchanged (Duke), impaling, Gules a saltire or, on a chief or three lions rampant gules (Holt)
Crest: A demi-lion rampant or holding an apple gules   Mantling: Gules and argent   Motto: Gloria Deo soli   Cherub's head at each top angle of shield
For Richard Southby, who m. Ann Holt, and d. 18 Mar. 1791.
(Gents. Mag. 286; M.I.)

2. All black background
On a lozenge surmounted by a cherub's head
Arms: As 1.
Skull below
For Ann, widow of Richard Southby, d. 1 Apr. 1795, aged 66. (M.I.)

3. All black background
On a lozenge surmounted by a cherub's head
Qly, 1st and 4th, Southby, 2nd and 3rd, Duke
Probably for Mary, 2nd dau. of Richard and Ann Southby, d. 7 Feb. 1835, aged 72. (M.I.)

4. All black background
Qly, 1st and 4th, Southby, 2nd and 3rd, Duke
Crest, mantling and motto: As 1.
Probably for Richard Duke Southby, who d. 1791, aged 33.

5. All black background
On a lozenge surmounted by a cherub's head
Azure on a bend cotised or between six lozenges argent each charged with an escallop sable six escallops vert (Pollen)   In pretence: Qly, 1st and 4th, Southby, 2nd and 3rd, Duke
For Charity Anne, dau. of Richard and Ann Southby, who m. Sir John Pollen, 1st Bt. (d. 17 Aug. 1814), and d. 30 July 1830, aged 75. (B.P. 1949 ed.; M.I.)

CASTLE COMBE

1. Sinister background black
Qly, 1st and 4th, Azure a bend or, on a canton argent a cross crosslet sable (Scrope), 2nd, Argent a fret between four crescents sable (Buncombe), 3rd, Sable three swords in pile argent hilted or a crescent argent for difference (Poulett), impaling, Qly, 1st and 4th, Azure a bend or (Scrope), 2nd, Argent a fess between four barrulets gules (Badlesmere), 3rd, Argent a saltire engrailed gules (Tiptoft)
Crest: From a ducal coronet or a plume of feathers charged with a cross crosslet argent   Mantling: Gules and argent   Motto: In caelo quies
For Emma, dau. of William Scrope, of Castle Combe, who m. 1821, George Poulett Thomson, who thereupon assumed the name and arms of Scrope in lieu of Thomson: she d.s.p. Aug. 1866.
(B.L.G. 2nd ed.; M.I.)

CHILTON FOLIAT

1. All black background
Qly, 1st and 4th, Argent on a chief gules two stags' heads cabossed or (Popham), 2nd and 3rd, Azure six lions rampant three, two and one argent (Leyborne), impaling, Sable a saltire between four cross crosslets argent (Andrew)
Crest: A stag's head couped or   Mantling: Gules and argent
Motto: Mens pristina mansit
For General Edward William Leyborne Popham, who m. 1806, Elizabeth, dau. of the Ven. John Andrew, Rector of Powderham, Devon, and d. 16 June 1843.   (B.L.G. 1937 ed.; M.I.)

2. Dexter background black
Qly, 1st and 4th, Argent a chevron gules surmounted by another ermine between three laurel slips each of three leaves vert (Cooper), 2nd, Argent a chevron gules between three cross crosslets fitchy sable within a double tressure flory counterflory gules (Kennedy), 3rd, Argent a bend between six lions rampant azure (Franks), impaling, Qly, 1st and 4th, Gules a lion couchant argent between six cross crosslets or (Tynte), 2nd and 3rd, Vert on a chevron argent three pheons sable (Kemeys)
Crest: A cubit arm erect the hand grasping a wreath of laurel proper
Mantling: Gules and argent   Motto (over crest): Virtute
Supporters: Dexter, A greyhound argent   Sinister, A stag proper
The shield is surrounded by the ribbon of a baronet of Nova Scotia with a badge pendent from it
For Sir William Cooper, 5th Bt., of Gogar, who m. 1827, Anne, dau. of Charles Kemeys Kemeys-Tynte, of Halsewell House, Somerset, and d. 14 Jan. 1837. (B.P. 1949 ed., Lord Wharton)

CHIRTON

1. Dexter background black
Qly, 1st and 4th, Argent on a bend sable three eagles displayed or (Ernle), 2nd and 3rd, Sable two bars and in chief three roundels argent (Hungerford),
Crest: A man's head couped at the shoulders head in profile proper wearing a long cap barry of six or and sable tasselled or   Mantling: Gules and argent
Unidentified

2. Sinister background black
Per fess or and argent a lion rampant azure (Yerbury, for Warriner), impaling, Barry of ten sable and argent, on a bend sable three eagles displayed or (Ernle)
Crest: A demi-lion or   Mantling: Gules and argent
For Elizabeth, dau. of Sir John Ernle, Bt., who m. 1739, as his 1st wife, Gifford Warriner, and d. 15 Dec. 1757. (B.L.G. 1853 ed.; M.I.; V.C.H.)

3. Dexter background black
Yerbury   In pretence: Argent on a bend sable three eagles displayed or (Ernle)   Also impaling, Sable a lion rampant between eight cross crosslets argent (Long)
Crest and mantling: As 2.   Motto: Mors janua vitæ
For Gifford Warriner, who m. 2nd, Anne, dau. of Richard Long, of Rood Ashton, and d. 1787. (Sources, as 2.)

4. All black background
On a lozenge   Yerbury   In pretence: Ernle, as 3. Also impaling Long
For Anne, widow of Gifford Warriner, d.s.p. Sept. 1815. (Sources, as 2.)
(Gifford Warriner's grandmother was heiress of Gifford Yerbury, d.s.p. 1712).

5. Dexter background black
Qly, 1st and 4th, Gules a fess chequy or and ermine between two antelopes courant argent armed or, in dexter chief a crescent argent for difference in 1st quarter only (Warriner), 2nd and 3rd, Ernle, as 3., impaling, Or
Crest: From a crown palisado azure a demi-eagle displayed or semy of crescents azure, a crescent gules for difference   Mantling: Gules and argent   Motto: Decus aemulatus avitum
Unidentified

CODFORD ST PETER

1. Dexter background black
Two oval shields, the dexter overlapping the sinister   Dexter, within the Garter, Qly, 1st and 4th, England, 2nd, Scotland, 3rd, Ireland, in chief a label of three points argent charged on the centre with a cross gules and on the outer points with a heart gules   In pretence: Saxony   Sinister, within an ornamental wreath, Qly of nine, 1st and 9th, Argent a cross moline gules (Pyrmont, 1st covered by dexter shield), 2nd and 8th, Argent three escutcheons gules (Rappolstein), 3rd and 7th, Argent three ravens' heads couped proper ducally crowned or (Hoheneck), 4th, covered by dexter shield, 5th, covered by escutcheon, 6th, Argent billetty azure a lion rampant gules crowned or (Geroldseck); over all an escutcheon, Or a molet of eight points sable (Waldeck)
Royal duke's coronet above
A small rectangular hatchment painted on silk, elaborately framed
For H.R.H. Prince Leopold, K.G., Duke of Albany, who d. 28 Mar. 1884.
(There is another hatchment, of normal shape, for Prince Leopold at Boyton)

COOMBE BISSETT

1. All black background
Vairy argent and gules on a canton or a buck's head cabossed proper (Becher)
Crest: A demi-lion rampant argent holding in its paws a bezant
Mantling: Gules and argent, ending in gold tassels
Unidentified

DAUNTSEY

1. All black background
Argent a chevron between three estoiles of six points sable (Mordaunt)
Earl's coronet   Motto: Nec placida contenta quiete est
Supporters: Two eagles rising argent armed or
For Charles, 5th Earl of Peterborough, who d. unm. 16 June 1814.
(Complete Peerage)

DRAYCOT CERNE

1. All black background
Qly, 1st, Gules a cross between twenty roundels argent (Wellesley), 2nd, Sable a lion rampant within an orle of eight cross crosslets argent

(Long), 3rd, Argent a chevron between three griffins' heads erased gules langued azure (Tylney), 4th, Azure a lion rampant argent within an orle of seven fleurs-de-lys or (Pole)
Earl's coronet   Crests: 1. From a ducal coronet or a demi-lion rampant gules holding a pennon of St George (Wellesley) 2. A lion's head erased argent in its mouth a hand gules (Long) 3. From a ducal coronet or a demi-lion rampant argent (Long) 4. From a ducal coronet or and a plume of feathers argent a griffin's head gules (Tylney) 5. A lion's gamb erased erect gules (Pole)   Motto: Porro unum est necessarium   Supporters: Two lions rampant gules each ducally gorged and chained or
For William Pole-Tylney-Long- Wellesley, 5th Earl of Mornington, d. 25 July 1863. (M.I.)

ENFORD

1. Dexter background black
Ermine on a chevron engrailed gules three escallops or (Grove), impaling, Gules a talbot passant or a chief ermine (Chafin)
Crest: A talbot passant sable collared argent   Mantling: Gules and argent
For John Grove, who m. 1686, Mary, dau. of William Chafin, of Zeals, and d. 1699. (B.L.G. 5th ed.; church guide)

2. All black background
On a lozenge surmounted by a winged skull
Ermine on a chevron engrailed gules an escallop or between two argent (Grove), impaling, Gules a talbot passant or a chief ermine (Chafin)
Winged skull below   Frame decorated with skulls and crossbones
For Mary, widow of John Grove, bur. 31 Mar. 1724. (Sources, as 1.)

3. All black background
Grove, as 2., impaling, Sable on a chevron between three greyhounds statant argent three trees eradicated proper (Naish)
Crest and mantling: As 1.   Motto: Mors janua vitæ   Frame decorated with skulls and crossbones
For Hugh Grove, son of John and Mary Grove, who m. 1721, Anne, dau. of Edward Naish of Bristol, bur. 12 Nov. 1765. (Sources, as 1.)

EVERLEIGH

1. All black background
Qly, 1st and 4th, Azure a cinquefoil ermine, in sinister chief of first quarter the Badge of Ulster (Astley), 2nd and 3rd, Ermine on a bend sable two cubit arms vested argent emerging from clouds the hands proper rending a horseshoe argent (Borlase)   In pretence: Gules a saltire or over all a cross engrailed argent (Prynce)

Crest: From a ducal coronet or a plume of three feathers gules
Mantling: Gules and argent   Motto: Fide sed cui vide
For Sir John Astley, 2nd Bt., who m. Mary, dau. and heir of Francis
Prynce, and d. 29 Dec. 1771. (B.E.B.)

2. **Sinister background black**
Azure a cinquefoil ermine within a bordure engrailed or (Astley),
impaling, Qly, 1st and 4th, Sable on a fess between three dragons' heads
erased or three estoiles of six points gules (Buckler), 2nd and 3rd,
Argent three stirrups proper within a bordure sable charged with
roundels argent (Gifford)   Cherub's head above
For Mary, dau. and co-heir of William Buckler, of Boreham, who m.
1755, as his 1st wife, Francis Dugdale Astley, of Everleigh, and d. 23
Sept. 1804. (B.P. 1949 ed.)
(This hatchment, recorded in 1952, is now missing)

3. **All black background**
Azure a cinquefoil ermine (Astley), impaling two coats per fess, in
chief, Qly, 1st and 4th, Sable on a fess between three dragons' heads
erased or three molets sable (Buckler), 2nd and 3rd, Azure three stirrups
or within a bordure argent charged with ten roundels sable (Gifford),
and in base, Qly, 1st and 4th, Azure a chevron between three swans'
heads erased argent (Geast), 2nd and 3rd, Argent a cross moline gules
charged with a Garter's coronet, in dexter chief a roundel gules
(Dugdale)
Crest: From a ducal coronet or a plume of three feathers argent
Mantling: Gules and argent   Motto: Fide sed cui vide
For Francis Dugdale Astley, who m. 2nd, 1805, Anne, dau. of Henry
Geast, and d. 26 Apr. 1818. (Battersby MS; B.P. 1949 ed.)

4. **Sinister background black**
Azure a cinquefoil ermine, in dexter chief the Badge of Ulster (Astley),
impaling, Azure a fess dancetty between three martlets or (Page)
Motto: Resurgam   Cherub's head above
For Sarah, dau. of William Page, who m. 1803, Sir John Dugdale Astley,
1st Bt., and d. 30 Aug. 1824. (B.P. 1949 ed.; M.I.)

5. **All black background;**
Azure a cinquefoil ermine within a bordure argent (Astley)
Crest: From a ducal coronet or a plume of three feathers argent
Mantling: Gules and argent
Unidentified
(This hatchment, recorded in 1952, is now missing)

FARLEY

1. **Dexter background black**
Two oval shields, each surmounted by a coronet, the dexter for a

Wiltshire

baron, the sinister for a baroness   Dexter shield, Ermine on a chevron azure three foxes' heads erased or, on a canton azure a fleur-de-lys or, in chief a crescent gules for difference (Fox), impaling, Qly, 1st and 4th, Qly France and England, 2nd, Scotland, 3rd, Ireland, all within a bordure compony argent and gules charged with eight roses gules (Dukedom of Richmond)   Sinister shield, as sinister of dexter shield
Crest: On a chapeau azure and ermine a fox sejant or   Mantle: Gules and argent   Motto: Re e marito   Supporters: Two foxes argent collared as the bordure in the arms, the sinister chained or   Winged skull in base
For Henry Fox, cr. Baron Holland of Foxley, co. Wilts, 16 Apr. 1763, who m. 1744, Georgiana Caroline (cr. Baroness Holland of Holland, co. Lincs, 6 May 1762), eldest dau. of Charles, 2nd Duke of Richmond, and d. 1 July 1774. (B.E.P.)

2. All black background
A shield and lozenge, each surmounted by a coronet, as 1.   Shield, Fox impaling, Richmond, as 1. Lozenge, Richmond arms only
Motto: As 1.   Supporters: As 1.   Cherub's head above and winged skull below
For Georgiana Caroline, Baroness Holland, d. 24 July 1774. (B.E.P.)

3. Dexter background black
Fox, as 1., but no crescent, impaling, Barry of six or azure, on a bend engrailed sable cotised gules three escallops or (Cave)
Crest: As 1.   Mantle: Gules and argent   Motto: Resurgam
Probably for Charles James Fox, the eminent statesman, son of Baron and Baroness Holland, who m. Mrs. Elizabeth Bridget Armistead (née Cane), and d. 15 Sept. 1806. She d. 8 July 1842. (B.E.B.; D.N.B.)

4. Dexter two-thirds background black
Three coats per pale   Qly, 1st and 4th, Sable two lions passant paly of six argent and gules (Strangways), 2nd and 3rd, Fox as 3., impaling to dexter, Per pale gules and sable three lions passant guardant in pale or (O'Grady), and to sinister, Qly, 1st and 4th, Azure a fleur-de-lys argent (Digby), 2nd and 3rd, Argent a saltire gules (Fitzgerald)
Earl's coronet   Crest: As 1.   Motto: Faire sans dire   Supporters: Two foxes, the dexter ermine fretty or collared dovetailed sable flory or; the sinister proper collared as dexter
For Henry Thomas, 2nd Earl of Ilchester, who m. 1st, 1772, Mary Theresa (d. 14 June 1790), dau. of Standish O'Grady, and 2nd, 1794, Maria (d. 23 Sept. 1842), dau. of the Very Rev. and Hon. William Digby, Dean of Durham, and d. 5 Sept. 1802.
(B.P. 1949 ed.)

HARTHAM, nr Corsham

1. Sinister background black
Pily counterpily of four traits or and sable the points ending in crosses formy two in chief and one in base, in centre chief a castle sable and in base two martlets or, on a chief azure a key erect ward upwards and to the sinister or between to the dexter a rose or and to the sinister a fleur-de-lys argent (Poynder)   In pretence: Ermine a fess indented paly vert and or between in chief two horses' heads erased sable and in base three arrows points downwards sable one in pale surmounted by two in saltire (Edmeades)   Two cherubs' heads above shield
For Mary Anne Edmeades, who m. Thomas Henry Allen Poynder, and d. 23 Oct. 1871. (M.I., Anthony Grigg)

2. All black background
Poynder, as 1., but rose argent barbed vert and seeded or   In pretence: Ermine a fess indented paly vert and or between in chief two unicorns' heads erased azure armed argent and in base three spears or points downwards azure one in pale surmounted by two in saltire (Edmeades)
Crest: From a tower argent charged with a cross flory gules a cubit arm vested sable cuffed or charged with a key as in the arms, the hand proper holding a cross formy fitchy argent   Mantling: Gules and argent   Motto: In Christo spes et gloria
For Thomas Henry Allen Poynder, who d. 26 Nov. 1873.
(Sources, as 1.)

HIGHWORTH

1. All black background
Per fess embattled argent and sable six crosses formy counterchanged (Warneford)   In pretence: Sable an inescutcheon within an orle of eight martlets argent (Calverley)
Crest: A garb or   Mantling: Gules and argent   Motto: Cruce quam muro tutior
For Col. Francis Warneford, of Warneford Place, who m. Catherine, dau. of Samuel Calverley, of Ewell Castle, Surrey, and d. 3 Feb. 1784, aged 51. (B.L.G. 1937 ed.; M.I.)

2. Dexter background black
Per fess embattled azure and argent six crosses formy counterchanged (Warneford), impaling, two coats per fess, in chief, Gules three towers proper (   ), and in base, Argent three roundels gules between two chevronels sable all between three choughs holding in their beaks sprays of leaves all proper (Flower)
Crest: A garb or   Mantling: Gules and argent   Motto: Cruce quam muro tutior   Winged skull below

Wiltshire

For Francis Warneford, who m. 1789, Elizabeth, eldest dau. of William, 2nd Viscount Ashbrook, and d. 27 Oct. 1835, aged 74. (Sources, as 1.)

3. All black background
On a lozenge   Argent two lions passant guardant sable, on a chief indented sable three covered cups or (Wetherell), impaling, Per fess embattled sable and argent six crosses formy counterchanged (Warneford)
Sprays of leaves, tied with a bow of red ribbon, flanking lozenge
For Harriet Elizabeth, dau. of Francis Warneford, who m. 1838, as his 2nd wife, Sir Charles Wetherell, and d. 8 Dec. 1864. (B.L.G. 1937 ed.)

4. All black background (should be sinister background black)
Argent a fess between three pheons sable (Rowden), impaling, Wetherell
Mantling: Gules and argent   Sprays of leaves, tied with a bow of gold ribbon, flanking shield   Cherub's head above
For Elizabeth, dau. of the Very Rev. Nathan Wetherell, who m. 1812, as his 1st wife, the Rev. Edward Rowden, Vicar of Highworth, and d. 9 Sept. 1825, aged 36. He d. 27 Mar. 1869, aged 89. (B.L.G. 1937 ed.; M.I.)

HILMARTON

1. All black background (actually grey-green)
Qly, 1st and 4th, Gules a chevron ermine between ten crosses formy six and four argent (Berkeley), 2nd and 3rd, Or a saltire engrailed sable (Botetourt)
Baron's coronet   Crest: A unicorn gules   Mantling: Gules and ermine   Motto: Resurgo rege favente   Supporters: Dexter, the figure of Prudence holding in her right hand a mirror proper
Sinister, the figure of Peace holding in her left hand a palm branch proper and in her right hand a bridle and bit proper   Frame decorated with skull and crossbones
For Norborne Berkeley, Baron Botetourt, who d. unm. 15 Oct. 1770. (Complete Peerage)

2. Dexter background black
Qly, 1st and 4th, Or on a canton sable a tiger's head erased or (Jacob), 2nd and 3rd, Qly argent and sable on a bend gules three molets argent (Calley), impaling, Argent a fess dancetty between three roses gules seeded argent barbed vert (Smith)
Crest: A tiger passant sable resting paw on an escutcheon or
Mantling: Gules and argent   Motto: Vivit post funera virtus   Frame decorated with skulls and crossbones
For John Jacob, who m. Mary, dau. of Matthew Smith, and d. 15 Mar. 1728, aged 77. (Tockenham par. regs, and M.I. in Hilmarton church)

3. **Sinister background black**
Qly, 1st and 4th, Jacob, 2nd and 3rd, Calley, impaling, Or three escallops in pale or (? Symes)
Crest and mantling: As 2.
Unidentified

4. **All black background**
Pily counterpily of five traits or and sable, the points ending in crosses formy two in chief and one in base, in fess point a tower sable (Poynder), impaling, Gules a bend ermine cotised indented or (Wykes)
Crest: Out of a tower argent charged with a cross patonce gules a cubit arm erect habited azure cuffed or the hand proper holding a cross formy fitchy or   Mantling: Gules and argent   Motto: Resurgam
For Thomas Poynder, who m. 1775, Mary, dau. of Edward Wix, and d. 1837. (Anthony Grigg)

5. **All black background**
Pily counterpily of five traits or and sable, the points ending in crosses formy two in chief and one in base, in fess point a tower sable and in base two martlets or, on a chief azure a key erect the wards upwards and to the sinister or between a rose on the dexter and a fleur-de-lys on the sinister argent (Poynder), impaling, Qly argent and gules on the second and third quarters a pheon argent (Cooper)
Crest and mantling: As 4.   Motto: In Christos spes et gloria
For Thomas Poynder, who m. Sarah Marianne, dau. of Capt. Allen Cooper, and d. 18 June 1856. She d. 11 Sept. 1838. (M.I.; Anthony Grigg)

HOLT

1. **All black background**
Azure a fess engrailed ermine between three talbots' heads erased or (Burton)
Crest: On a mural coronet argent a beacon fired proper   Mantling: Gules and argent   Motto: Mors janua vitæ
For James Burton, who d. 19 Mar. 1812, aged 82. Maria Susanna, his wife, d. 2 July 1786, aged 46. (M.I.)

2. **Dexter background black**
Azure a fess between three leopards' faces jessant-de-lys or (Watkin), impaling, Argent three saddles sable (Hervey)
Crest: A leopard's face jessant-de-lys or   Mantling: Gules and argent   Motto: Mors janua vitæ
For the Rev. John Burton Watkin, Vicar of Marshfield, Lord of the Manor of Holt, who m. Barbara, dau. of the Rev. Edward Hervey, of Hulcote, Beds, and d. 20 Mar. 1822, aged 76. She d. 6 Dec. 1836, aged 83. (M.I.)

KILMINGTON

1. Sinister background black
Qly, 1st and 4th, Azure three blocks argent each charged with an annulet sable (Paynter), 2nd and 3rd, Sable three swords in pile argent hilted or (Paulet), impaling, Qly of three, per pale and per fess, 1st, Ermine five chevronels argent between three martlets sable (Drew), 2nd, Gules a pale or (   ), 3rd, Ermine three annulets interlaced or (   ) Shield held by an angel standing behind it
Motto: Arumnarum requies mors
For Caroline, dau. of Comm. Edward Drew. who m. 1866, George William Paynter, and d. 11 Jan. 1894. (B.L.G. 1937 ed.; M.I.)

2. All black background
Arms: As 1.
Crest: Three broken arrows or, points downwards two in saltire one in pale, banded gules   Mantling: Gules and argent   Motto: Resurgam
For George William Paynter, who d. 24 Nov. 1906. (Sources, as 1.)

3. Sinister background black
Qly, 1st and 4th, Paynter, 2nd, Paulet, 3rd, Or three roundels gules a label of three points azure (Courtenay)   In pretence: Drew qly as 1.
Also impaling, Or on a fess between three lions rampant gules six roundels sable (Yonge)
Shield supported by two angels proper dexter winged gules sinister azure   Motto: In coelo quies
For Mary Josephine, dau. of William Francis Von Moevis Yonge, who m. 1901, Charles Paulet Camborne Paynter, and d. 17 Apr. 1911. (Sources, as 1.)

4. All black background
Arms: As 3.
Crest and mantling: As 2.   Motto: Mors janua vitæ
For Charles Paulet Camborne Paynter, who d. 1 Jan. 1947, aged 68. (Sources, as 1.)

LACOCK Abbey

1. Dexter background black
Qly, 1st and 4th, Argent on a fess azure three lozenges or (Feilding), 2nd and 3rd, Or a lion rampant gules ducally crowned sable (Hapsburg), impaling, Qly, 1st and 4th, Sable two lions passant paly of six argent and gules (Strangways), 2nd, Ermine on a chevron azure three foxes' heads erased or, on a canton azure a fleur-de-lys or (Fox), 3rd, Sable three talbots passant argent (Horner)
Shield borne on the Austrian Eagle displayed sable, and above it a cap of a Count of the Austrian Empire

Crest: The Austrian Eagle displayed sable bearing on its breast a shield charged with the arms of Feilding   No mantling: Motto: Crescit sub pondere virtus
For Admiral Charles Feilding, who m. 1804, Elizabeth Theresa, dau. of Henry Thomas, 2nd Earl of Ilchester, and widow of William Davenport Talbot, of Lacock Abbey, and d. 2 Sept. 1837. (B.P. 1949 ed.)
(This hatchment, recorded in 1954, in the Estate outbuildings, is now missing)

LANGLEY BURRELL

1. All brown background
Argent two chevronels sable (Ashe), impaling, Gules two bars argent (Martyn)
Crest: A cockatrice or, combed, wattled and armed gules   Mantling: Gules and argent   Motto: Resurgam
For Robert Ashe, son of the Rev. Robert Ashe, who m. Thermuthis, dau. of Samuel Martyn of Kennet, and d. 9 Dec. 1829. She d. 21 Dec. 1823. (M.I.; B.L.G. 5th ed.)

2. All black background
Ashe, impaling, Per fess argent and or a lion rampant per fess sable and gules, in chief two dexter hands couped gules (Daly)
Crest: As 1.   Mantling: Sable and argent   Motto: As 1.
For the Rev. Robert Martyn Ashe, who m. 1852, Letitia, dau. of Capt. Arthur Daly, and d. 18 Jan. 1885. She d. 17 Dec. 1884. (Sources, as 1.)

LONGBRIDGE DEVERILL

1. All black background
Two shields   Dexter, within the Garter, Qly, 1st and 4th, Barry of ten or and sable (Thynne), 2nd and 3rd, Argent a lion rampant tail nowed and erect gules (Boteville)   Sinister, within an ornamental wreath, as dexter, impaling, Qly sable and argent in the first quarter a lion rampant argent (Byng)
Marquess's coronet   Crest: A reindeer statant or   Motto: J'ay bonne cause   Supporters: Dexter a reindeer or collared sable Sinister, A lion tail erect and nowed gules
For Thomas, 2nd Marquess of Bath, who m. 1794, Isabella Elizabeth, 3rd dau. of George, 4th Viscount Torrington, and d. 27 Mar. 1837. (B.P. 1949 ed.)

LUDGERSHALL

1. Dexter background black
Qly, 1st, Or on a bend engrailed gules three cross crosslets fitchy argent

(Richmond), 2nd, Argent a cross flory azure between four molets pierced of six points gules, in dexter chief a crescent sable for difference (Webb), 3rd, Azure on a bend between six lozenges or each charged with an escallop sable three escallops sable (Pollen), 4th, Argent on a bend sable three annulets or (St Loe)   In pretence: Ermine on a bend sable two cubit arms vested azure cuffed argent issuant from clouds the hands proper rending a horseshoe or (Borlase) Also impaling, Argent on a chevron gules three towers argent, on a canton azure a fleur-de-lys or (Vilett)
Crest: A tilting spear argent in three pieces, one erect point downwards the other two in saltire, enfiled with a ducal coronet or   Mantling: Gules and argent   Motto: Moriendo vivo
For Lieut.-General John Richmond Webb, cr. a Knight of the Order of Generosity by the King of Prussia, who m. 1st, Henrietta, dau. of William Borlase, M.P. for Marlow, and 2nd, Anne Skeate, granddaughter of Thomas Vilett of Swindon. He was bur. 9 Sept. 1724.
(Ped. by Sir Thomas Phillipps, Bodleian: D.N.B.)

2. All black background
Gules a chevron paly of ten azure and or between three molets argent (Everett), impaling, Chequy or and ermine a lion rampant gules, on a chief sable a leopard's face between two cross crosslets fitchy or (Cooke)
Crest: A griffin's head erased sable beaked gules charged with three barrulets one or between two argent   Mantling: Gules and argent
Motto: Resurgam
Unidentified

LYDIARD TREGOZE

1. All black background
Argent on a chief gules two molets or (St John)
Viscount's coronet   Crest: A falcon rising or   Motto: Nil admirari
Supporters: Two falcons wings elevated or, ducally crowned gules, each charged on the breast with the Hames   Winged skull below
For Frederick, 3rd Viscount St John and 2nd Viscount Bolingbroke, who m. 1757, Diana, eldest dau. of Charles, 3rd Duke of Marlborough, whom he divorced 1768, and d. 5 May 1787. (B.P. 1949 ed.)

2. Sinister background black
St John, impaling, Gules on a bend or three martlets sable within a bordure ermine (Collins)
Viscountess's coronet   Mantling: Gules and argent   Motto: In coelo quies   Supporters: Dexter, A falcon wings elevated or, ducally gorged gules   Sinister as dexter, but not ducally gorged, and charged on the breast with the Hames

For Charlotte, dau. of the Rev. Thomas Collins, of Winchester, who m. 1783, as his 1st wife, George Richard, 4th Viscount St John and 3rd Viscount Bolingbroke, and d. 11 Jan. 1803. (B.P. 1949 ed.)

The following three armorial boards are all rectangular; they will be included in the final volume, which will deal with transitional examples, but in view of the special interest of the St John memorials they are also included here.

3. All brown background
Argent on a chief gules two molets or a crescent for difference (St John)   A wood panel, c. 2 ft x 1½ ft
Probably for Walter St John, who was drowned in a bathing accident on 18 Aug. 1597.

4. Sinister background black
Qly of eight, 1st, Argent on a chief gules two pierced molets or, a crescent sable for difference, the Badge of Ulster (St John), 2nd, Gules a fess between six martlets or, a pierced molet sable for difference (Beauchamp), 3rd, Argent a fess sable between three crescents gules (Pateshull), 4th, Paly of six argent and azure, on a bend gules three eagles displayed or (Grandison), 5th Or two bars gemel and in chief a lion passant gules (Tregoz), 6th, Argent a fess gules between three estoiles of six points sable (Ewyas), 7th, Sable two bars and in chief three roundels argent (Hungerford), 8th, Per pale indented gules and vert a chevron or (Heytesbury), impaling, Qly of eight, 1st, Qly per fess indented gules and or (Leighton), 2nd, Azure three escallops or (Malet), 3rd, Gules a fess between six pears or (Clopton), 4th, Or three bendlets gules (   ), 5th, Argent a crow proper (Corbet), 6th, Argent three boars' heads couped sable (Cambray), 7th, Azure a cross moline voided or (Knollys), 8th, Gules on a chevron argent three roses gules barbed and seeded proper (Knollys)
A wood panel, c. 2 ft x 1½ ft
For Anne, dau. of Sir Thomas Leighton, of Feckenham, Worcester, who m. as his 1st wife, Sir John St John, 1st Bt., and d. 19 Sept. 1628. (B.P. 1949 ed.; M.I.)

5. All black background
Argent on a chevron engrailed between three estoiles of six points sable three bucks' heads cabossed argent (Ayliffe), impaling, Argent on a chief gules two molets or, in fess point a crescent sable for difference (St John) A wood panel, c. 1¾ ft x 1¼ ft
For Sir George Ayliffe, who m. Anne, dau. of Sir John St John, and was bur. 6 Dec. 1643. (Bishop's Transcripts)
(The 'hatchment' of Lady Ayliffe is at Brinkworth)

MALMESBURY

1. Dexter background black
Qly, 1st and 4th, Argent a chevron azure between three squirrels gules each cracking a nut proper (Lovell), 2nd and 3rd, Or on a chevron between three leopards's faces gules three trefoils slipped argent (Harvey), impaling, Argent a chevron between three molets sable (Willes)
Crest: A squirrel cracking a nut proper   Mantling: Gules and argent
Motto: Resurgam
For Peter Harvey Lovell, of Cole Park, who m. Charlotte, 4th dau. of the Ven. William Willes, Archdeacon of Wells, and d. 20 Jan. 1841, aged 81. (B.L.G. 1937 ed.; M.I.)
(This hatchment, recorded in 1952, is now missing)

MARKET LAVINGTON

1. Dexter background black
Qly of three (tierced), 1st, Per fess or and argent an eagle displayed sable on the breast an escutcheon gules charged with a bend vair, in chief a crescent sable for difference (Bouverie), 2nd, Gules a bend vair (Bouverie), 3rd, Argent a bend gules gutty argent between two choughs proper a chief chequy or and sable (Pleydell), impaling, Gules a fess between eight billets or (May)
Crest: A double-headed eagle ducally gorged or charged with a cross crosslet argent   Mantling: Gules and argent   Motto: Patria cara carior libertas
For the Hon. Duncombe Pleydell-Bouverie, who m. 1809, Louisa, 2nd dau. of Joseph May, and d. 5 Nov. 1850. (B.P. 1949 ed.)

2. All black background
On a lozenge   Arms: As 1.
For Louisa, widow of the Hon. Duncombe Pleydell-Bouverie, d. 6 June 1852. (B.P. 1949 ed.)

3. All black background
Or three martlets sable, on a chief sable a sun in splendour proper (Merewether), impaling, Sable a chevron ermine between three escallops argent (   )
Crest: A gauntlet proper grasping a sword argent hilted or entwined with a snake proper   Mantling: Gules and argent
Unidentified

MELKSHAM

1. All black background
Argent on a cross sable ermined argent a leopard's face or (Bruges),

impaling, Azure on a fess argent three saltires couped gules (Gale)
Crest: An anchor erect or   Mantling: Gules and argent   Motto:
Mihi coelum portus
For Thomas Bruges, who m. Sarah, and d. 1 Jan. 1835. She d. 23 Feb.
1801. (M.I.)
(There is another hatchment for Thomas Bruges at Seend)

MERE

1. **Dexter background black**
Qly, 1st and 4th, Gules a talbot passant or a chief ermine (Chafin),
2nd, Azure a chevron between three escallops or (Erlegh), 3rd, Argent
on a bend gules three lozenges argent in sinister chief a trefoil slipped
gules (Marsh), impaling, Sable two bars and in chief three molets or
(Freke)
Crest: A talbot passant or   Mantling: Gules and argent
For William Chafin, who m. Mary, dau. of Thomas Freke of
Hannington, and d. 13 May 1695, aged 55. She d. 27 Oct. 1712, aged
79. (M.I.)

2. **All black background**
Chafin arms only
Crest and mantling: As 1.   Motto: Mors janua vitæ
Possibly for Thomas Chafin, d.
(Colt Hoare, Hundred of Mere, 15, 37)

3. **Dexter background black**
Ermine on a chevron gules three escallops or (Grove), impaling, Grove
Crest: A talbot passant proper collared argent   Mantling: Gules and
argent   Motto: Ni dessus ni dessous
Probably for William Chafin Grove, who m. Elizabeth, dau. of John
Grove, of Ferne, and d.s.p. 17 Jan. 1793. (B.L.G. 5th ed.; Gents.
Mag., 93)

4. **Dexter background black**
Ermine on a chevron engrailed or three escallops argent (Grove),
impaling, Chequy argent and sable a fess gules (Acland)
Crest, mantling and motto: As 3.
For Charles Grove, M.D., who m. 1786, Elizabeth, dau. of Arthur
Acland, of Fairfield, Somerset, and d. 27 Oct. 1806, aged 59.
She d. 8 May 1843. (B.L.G. 5th ed.; M.I.)

5. **All black background**
On a lozenge   Ermine on a chevron engrailed gules an escallop or
between two argent (Grove), impaling, Argent a chevron azure between
seven boars' heads erect erased four and three vert each with in its

mouth a cross crosslet fitchy gules (Michell)
For Eleanor, dau. of Thomas Michell, of Standen, Hungerford, who m.
1819, William Chafin Grove, and d. Nov. 1862. (B.L.G. 5th ed.)

6. Dexter background black
Ermine on a chevron engrailed gules three escallops or (Grove)
Crest, mantling and motto: As 3.
Perhaps for the Rev. Thomas Grove, Vicar of Mere, who d.s.p. 21 Apr.
1809. (B.L.G. 5th ed.; M.I.)

7. All black background
Ermine on a chevron engrailed gules an escallop or between two argent
(Grove)
Crest and mantling: As 3.   Motto: Resurgam
Probably for the Rev. William Grove, of Zeals House, who d.s.p. 1768.
(B.L.G. 5th ed.; Colt Hoare MS.)

8. Sinister background black
Sable gutty argent three roses argent (Still), impaling, Azure two castles
and two lions rampant murally crowned in saltire argent (Skrine)
Motto: Mors janua vitæ   Cherub's head above and palm branches in
base
For Sarah, dau. of Richard Dickson Skrine, who m. Richard Still, and
d. 10 Feb. 1789, aged 32. He d. 16 May 1811, aged 57. (M.I.)

MILDENHALL

1. Dexter background black
Per fess argent and ermine three lions passant guardant sable (Calcraft),
impaling, Per fess sable and argent (   )
Crest: A greyhound per pale sable and argent   Mantling: Gules and
argent   Motto: In coelo quies
For General John Calcraft, Coldstream Guards, who d. 20 Feb. 1830,
aged 64. (M.I.)

2. All black background
Argent a chevron between three eagles displayed gules (Francis)
Crest: A dove rising argent, in the beak an olive branch proper
Mantling: Gules and argent   Motto: Resurgam
For the Rev. Charles Francis, 33 years Rector of Mildenhall, who d.
3 Oct. 1821, aged 70. (M.I.)

3. All black background
On a lozenge surmounted by a skull
Gules a fess between two chevrons argent (Nourse), impaling, Argent
on two bars sable three fleurs-de-lys two and one or (Hoet)

Hour glass in base
Perhaps for Hester Nourse, widow, who d. at Mildenhall, 7 Mar.
1712/13.
(Coll. Top. & Gen., v. 348)

ORCHESTON ST GEORGE

1. Dexter background black
Qly, 1st, Or six annulets three two and one sable (Lowther), 2nd,
Argent crusilly three fleurs-de-lys within a bordure engrailed sable
(Beresford), 3rd, Gules a chevron between three combs argent
(Ponsonby), 4th, Argent a chief azure over all a lion rampant gules
crowned or (St George), impaling, Or two bars wavy and in chief
three whales' heads erect erased sable (Colbeck)
Crest: A goose proper   Mantling: Gules and argent   Motto:
Resurgam
For the Rev. Chambre Brabazon Ponsonby Lowther, for seventeen
years rector of Orcheston, who d. 10 May 1830. (M.I.)

POTTERNE

1. All black background
Qly sable and argent in the first quarter a lion rampant argent (Byng),
impaling, Azure a swan standing on earth proper (   )
Crest: An antelope passant ermine, armed, maned and unguled or
A small hatchment, badly painted
Unidentified

PRESHUTE

1. All black background
Qly, 1st, Gules a chevron vair between three crescents argent
(Goddard), 2nd, Azure a fess indented between three eagles' heads
erased or (Goddard), 3rd, Argent on a fess gules a squirrel sejant or, in
chief per pale or and gules and in base three battleaxes or (   ), 4th
Sable three birds argent, impaling, two coats per fess, in chief, Argent
three choughs proper (   ), and in base, . . . on a bend . . . (   )
Crest: A stag's head cabossed argent   Mantling: Gules and argent
Motto: Cervus . . . . . rv . .
A small hatchment, on wood panel, c. 2 ft. x 2 ft, the frame decorated
with skulls, crossbones and hourglasses
Unidentified

2. Sinister background black
Qly, 1st and 4th, Argent a pale lozengy sable (Daniell), 2nd and 3rd,

Argent a heraldic tyger reguardant sable armed and langued gules
(Deresbury), impaling, Qly, 1st and 4th, Or a chevron between three
apples gules stalked proper (Southby), 2nd and 3rd, Sable a chevron
between three cronels argent (Wiseman)
Crests: Dexter, A unicorn's head argent armed and maned or
Sinister, indistinguishable   Mantling: Gules and argent
A small hatchment, on wood panel, c. 2 ft x 2 ft, the frame decorated
with skulls, crossbones and hourglasses
For Catherine, dau. of John Southby, of Carswell, who m. Jeffery
Daniell, and was bur. 7 Sept. 1648. (Vis. of Wiltshire; Coll. Top &
Gen. v. 348)

3. Sinister background black
Qly of eight, 1st and 8th, Daniell, 2nd, Deresbury, 3rd, Qly argent and
gules in the second and third quarters a fret or, over all a fess azure
(Norris), 4th, Gules six fleurs-de-lys or a crescent or for difference
(Norris), 5th, Sable a cross engrailed ermine (Duton), 6th, Argent six
lions rampant, three two and one sable (Savage), 7th, Argent a chevron
sable between three lapwings proper (Whittoxmead), over all a molet or
for difference, impaling, Qly of eight, 1st, Argent on a bend sable three
eagles displayed or (Ernle), 2nd, Argent a chevron gules between three
boars' heads erased sable armed or langued gules a crescent or on the
chevron for difference (Wroughton), 3rd, Gules three sheaves of as
many arrows, in each sheaf one in pale and two in saltire points
downwards headed and feathered or (Best), 4th, Ermine on a bend
azure three leopards' faces or (Cambride), 5th, Per pale sable and argent
a cross flory counterchanged (Malwin), 6th, Per chevron gules and
ermine three chessrooks counterchanged (Holwell), 7th, Ermine two
chevrons gules (Finamore), 8th, Argent a cross and in dexter chief a
fleur-de-lys sable (Haydock)
Crests: Dexter, as 2.   Sinister, A Saracen's head in profile proper
wearing a cap argent turned up or charged with three bendlets sinister
wavy or   Mantling: Gules and argent   Mottoes: My hope is my
comfort   Per aspera ad astra
A small hatchment, on wood panel, c. 2 ft x 2 ft, the frame decorated
with skulls, crossbones and hourglasses
For Rachel, dau. of John Ernle, of Whetham, who m. as his 2nd wife,
Jeffery Daniell, and was bur. 7 Oct. 1677. (Sources, as 2.)
(This hatchment was stolen from the church in 1970)

RUSHALL

1. All black background
Argent a fess azure between three molets gules, in dexter chief the
Badge of Ulster (Poore)

Crest: A cubit arm, erect, vested azure, slashed argent, cuffed ermine, the sleeve charged with two molets in fess or, the hand grasping an arrow proper   Mantling: Azure and argent   Also a mantle gules and ermine, edged and tasselled or   Motto: Honor fidei merces
A tilting spear in fess behind shield
For Sir John Methuen Poore, 1st Bt., who d. unm. 1 June 1820.
(B.P. 1868 ed.)

SALISBURY, St Edmund
(*All transferred, Nov. 1982, to St Thomas*)

1. Dexter background black
Azure a chevron between three lions' heads erased or (Wyndham), impaling, Argent a sun in splendour gules (Hearst)
Crest: A lion's head erased or within a fetterlock the bow chequy sable and or   Mantling: Gules and argent
For Wadham Wyndham, of St Edmund's College, Salisbury, who m. Sarah, dau. of William Hearst, and d. 19 Feb. 1736, aged 74.
(B.L.G. 1937 ed.; M.I.)

2. Sinister background black
Wyndham, impaling, Gules the trunk of a tree raguly in bend argent (Penruddocke)
Crest: A lion's head erased within a fetterlock or   Mantling: Gules and argent
For Arundel, dau. of Thomas Penruddocke, of Compton, who m. 1735, Henry Wyndham, of the Close, and d. 3 Sept. 1780. (Sources, as 1.)

3. Dexter background black
Qly, 1st and 4th, Wyndham, 2nd and 3rd, Hearst, impaling, Per fess argent and sable a pale counterchanged and three horses' heads erased sable, on a chief ermine two bombs or fired proper (Slade)
Crests: Dexter, A lion's head erased within a fetterlock or   Sinister, The sun rising from behind a grove of trees proper   Mantling: Gules and argent   Motto: Au bon droit   Hatchment inscribed on back: Mrs Pearce painted Nover 20th 1844.
For Wadham Wyndham, of the College, Salisbury, M.P. for Wilts, who m. Anne Eliza, dau. of Lieut.-General Slade, and d.s.p. 23 Oct. 1843.
(Sources, as 1.)

4. Sinister background black
Qly, 1st and 4th, Wyndham, 2nd and 3rd, Gyronny of eight or and sable a bordure argent charged with eight crescents sable (Campbell)
In pretence: Wyndham   Mantling: Gules and argent   Cherub's head above
Hatchment inscribed on back: W. & L. Pearce – Wm. Bailey Painter Dec. 19 1845.

For Caroline Frances, sister of Wadham Wyndham, who m. 1797, Lt.-Col. John Campbell of Dunoon, Argyll, and Blunham, Beds. They took in 1844 the surname of Campbell-Wyndham. She d. 3 Dec. 1845. (Sources, as 1.)

5. All black background
Qly, 1st and 4th, Azure a chevron between three lions' heads erased or a canton or (Wyndham), 2nd and 3rd, Campbell   In pretence: Wyndham (no canton)
Crests: Dexter, A lion's head erased within a fetterlock or charged with a cross crosslet sable   Sinister, Two oars of a galley in saltire or
Mantling: Gules and argent   Motto: Vis et fides   Hatchment inscribed on back: March 5th 1846. Wm. Bailey. Painter.
For John Campbell-Wyndham, who d. 12 Feb. 1846. (Sources, as 1.)

6. Sinister background black
Gules a lion rampant argent (   ), impaling, Argent a sun in splendour gules (Hearst)
Skull above
Unidentified

7. All black background
On a lozenge surmounted by a cherub's head
Qly, 1st and 4th, Azure a fess ermine in chief three fleurs-de-lys or (Kenton), 2nd and 3rd, Gules a lion rampant argent langued azure (   ), impaling, Argent on a chevron sable three quatrefoils or (Eyre)
Motto: In coelo quies
Unidentified

8. All black background
Gules on a fess argent three estoiles of six points or (Whitchurch), impaling, Argent a chevron between three molets gules (   )
Crest: An estoile of six points or   Mantling: Gules and argent
Motto: Resurgam
Unidentified

9. All light background
On a lozenge surmounted by a cherub's head
Vert a fess wavy between three lions passant or (Hawes)
Mantling: Gules and argent   Motto: Missis terrestribus superna peto
For Margaret Jane, sister of the Rev. Herbert Hawes, Rector of St Edmund's. She d. 31 July 1820. (M.I. in St Andrew's, Bemerton)

SALISBURY, St Martin

1. Dexter background black
Argent a tower between three keys two and one wards upwards and to

dexter sable (Baker), impaling, Sable a trefoil slipped between eight molets argent (Phipps)
Crest: From a tower sable an arm in armour embowed the hand proper holding a bar sable ended or   Mantling: Gules and argent   Motto: Non periit sed obdormivit
For Edward Baker, who m. Jane Phipps, and d. 1 Nov. 1796. (M.I.)

2. All black background
On a lozenge surmounted by a cherub's head
Arms: As 1., but six molets
Motto: Non in aeturnum moriar
For Jane, widow of Edward Baker, d. 10 Feb. 1800. (M.I.)

3. All black background
Argent a tower between three keys one and two wards downwards and to sinister sable (Baker)
Crest: From a tower sable an arm in armour embowed the hand proper holding a bar argent ended or   Mantling: Gules and argent   Motto: As 1.
For the Rev. Henry Baker, who d. 18 Oct. 1794, aged 22.
(Church guide)

4. Dexter background black
Qly, 1st and 4th, Argent three bars and a canton gules (Fuller), 2nd and 3rd, Sable a block argent (   ), impaling, Per chevron or and argent a lion rampant reguardant gules (   )
Crest: A beacon inflamed proper   Mantling: Gules and argent
Motto: Ante obitum nemo felix   Cherub's head at each top angle of shield   Skull in base
For John Fuller, who d. 28 Mar. 1777. (Church guide; Gents. Mag. 195)

5. All black background
On a lozenge surmounted by a cherub's head
Argent on a cross sable five crescents or (Thomas)
Motto: In coelo quies
For Mary Thomas, who d. 18 May 1781. (M.I.)

6. All black background
Qly, 1st and 4th, Argent a fess between six lions' heads erased gules (Gooding), 2nd and 3rd, qly i. Or a bend gules (Cottle), ii. Argent two bars and in chief a demi-griffin issuant sable (Cahurta), iii. Or a chevron gules between three leaves vert (Lisle), iv. Argent a griffin segreant sable (Griffin)
Motto: Esperans en Dieu   Shield flanked by palm branches and surmounted by an ornamental urn
Unidentified (Quarterings from MS in Salisbury Library)

Wiltshire

7. All black background
Argent a cross engrailed between four bats displayed sable (Batt), impaling, Gules three lions passant guardant or a label of three points argent (   )   Skull and hourglass above shield   A small hatchment on a wood panel
Possibly for John Batt, d. 1723. (Guide to church)

SALISBURY, St Thomas

1. Dexter background black
Sable a lion rampant between eight cross crosslets argent (Long), impaling, Argent a greyhound courant sable, on a chief indented sable three bezants (Blackall)
Crest: A demi-lion rampant argent   Mantling: Gules and argent
For Walter Long, of New Sarum, who m. 2nd, 1727, Philippa, dau. of John Blackall, of London, and d. 15 Jan. 1769. (B.L.G. 2nd ed.; M.I.)

2. All black background
On a lozenge surmounted by a cherub's head
Arms: As 1.
Motto: Mors janua vitæ
For Philippa, widow of Walter Long, d. 14 Mar. 1798. (Sources, as 1.)

3. All black background
On a lozenge surmounted by a cherub's head
Long arms only
Probably for Eleanor, dau. of Walter and Philippa Long, d. 15 Mar. 1824, aged 87. (M.I.)

4. Dexter background black
Azure three bulls' heads erased or (Hayter), impaling, Argent a lion rampant gules between three pheons sable (Egerton)
Crest: A bull's head erased or pierced through the neck with a spear and vulned proper   Mantling: Gules and argent   Motto: In coelo quies
For William Hayter, of Newton Toney, who m. Elizabeth, dau. of Scroop Egerton, and d. 23 July 1805. (M.I.)

5. Dexter background black
Sable a boar's head couped close in bend argent langued gules dripping blood proper (Spooner), impaling, Argent on a chevron gules between three bugle horns sable stringed gules three cross crosslets fitchy or (Burt)
Crest: A boar's head couped at the neck proper pierced in the neck with an arrow argent vulned proper   Mantling: Gules and argent
Motto: Mors janua vitæ

For Charles Spooner, of the Close, Salisbury, who m. 2nd, Mary Burt, and d. at Bath, 11 May 1790. (Franks Cat. of Bookplates; Salisbury Journal)

6. **Dexter background black**
Qly, 1st and 4th, Or two chevrons between three lions' gambs erased gules (Powell), 2nd and 3rd, Gules an eagle displayed ermine (Priaulx) In pretence: Gules the stump of a tree argent sprouting out branches or (Burroughes)
Crest: A lion's gamb erased or armed gules   Mantling: Gules and argent   Motto: In coelo quies
For Francis Powell, of Hurdcott House, who m. Anna Maria, dau. of Sydenham Burroughes, of New Sarum, and d. 24 Jan. 1786. (B.L.G. 2nd ed.; M.I.)

7. **All black background**
Azure a fess wavy between three lions passant or (Hawes), impaling, Sable on the sea proper a lion passant or in chief three bezants, on a canton or an escallop between two palmers' staves sable (Hawkins)
Crest: From a mural coronet sable a lion's head erased or   Mantling: Gules and argent   Motto: Missis terrestribus superna petimus
Probably for the Rev. John Hawes, Rector of Bemerton, who d. 26 Dec. 1787, aged 68. (M.I. in Bemerton church)

8. **All black background**
Argent on a chevron sable three quatrefoils or, in dexter chief a crescent sable for difference (Eyre), impaling, Eyre, no crescent
Crest: An armed leg couped at the thigh, garnished and spurred or
Mantling: Gules and argent   Motto: Sola virtus invicta
For John Eyre, of Landford, who m. his cousin, Elizabeth, dau. of Giles Eyre, of Ashley House, Box, and d. 1799. She d. 20 Mar. 1758. (B.L.G. 1937 ed.)

9. **All black background**
Qly, 1st and 4th, Eyre, no crescent, 2nd, Or three oak trees eradicated proper (Snelgrove), 3rd, Argent on a bend cotised sable three fusils ermine (Ryves)   In pretence: Azure three crescents argent each charged with an escallop gules (   )
Crest and mantling: As 8.   Motto: Post laborem requies
Unidentified

(*10. to 18. see St Edmund*)

SEEND

1. **All black background**
On an asymmetric lozenge surmounted by a cherub's head
Per chevron gules and sable two chevronels or each charged with seven

molets azure between in chief four escarbuncles and twelve escutcheons or and in base a lamb passant argent (Schomberg), impaling, Argent on a chief vert two spearheads argent embrued gules (Brodrick)
Mantling: Gules and argent   Motto: Deo duce
For Amelia, dau. of John Brodrick, who m. Isaac Schomberg, and d. 19 Apr. 1840, aged 74. He d. 20 Jan. 1813, aged 59. (M.I.)

2. Identical to Melksham 1. (q.v.)
For Thomas Bruges, who m. Sarah (Gale), and d. 1 Jan. 1835. (M.I. in Melksham church)

3. All black background
On a lozenge   Argent on a bend cotised azure three cinquefoils or (Awdry), impaling, Awdry
Crest: From a ducal coronet or a lion's head erased azure   Mantling: Gules and argent   Motto: Nil sine Deo
For Jane, dau. of John Awdry of Melksham, who m. 1724, Ambrose Awdry, of Seend, and d. 22 Aug. 1769. (B.L.G. 2nd ed.; M.I.)

4. Dexter background black
Awdry, impaling, Sable on a chevron between three human faces crowned or three fleurs-de-lys azure (Guy)
Crest, mantling and motto: As 3.
For Ambrose Awdry, of Seend, who m. Hannah, dau. of Anthony Guy, of Chippenham, and d.s.p. 15 June 1842. (B.L.G. 2nd ed.; M.I.)

SEVINGTON, nr Castle Combe

1. All black background
Per pale argent and azure a lion passant between three greyhounds' heads erased counterchanged (Neeld)
Crest: A wolf's head erased sable between two branches of palm proper
Motto: Extender factis
Probably for Joseph Neeld, of Grittleton, who built the village school in 1849, and d. 24 Mar. 1856. (Frederick Boase, Mod. Eng. Biog. vol. ii.)
(This hatchment is in the old village school, which was reputed at the time to be the smallest in England)

STANTON FITZWARREN

1. All black background
Sable two bendlets and three molets in pale or one between the bendlets (Hippisley), impaling, Per pale, paly of six argent and azure, and azure (Trenchard)

Crest: A cubit arm erect vested azure cuffed argent the hand proper holding a knife argent   Mantling: Gules and argent   Motto: Mors janua vitæ
For John Hippisley, of Stanton, who m. 1703, Frances, dau. of William Trenchard, of Cutteridge, and d. 9 Dec. 1738. (B.L.G. 1937 ed.; Gents. Mag. 660)

2. Sinister background black
Qly, 1st and 4th, Trenchard, 2nd and 3rd, Per fess or and argent, on a saltire engrailed sable five estoiles of five points argent (Ashfordby) In pretence: Gules three crescents qly gules and or, a canton or (Cooke)
Motto: In coelo quies   Cherub's head above shield
For Martha, dau. of William Croft Cooke, of London, who m. as his 1st wife, the Rev. John Ashfordby-Trenchard, and d. 27 Apr. 1833, aged 60. (M.I.; B.L.G. 1937 ed.)

3. Dexter background black
Qly, 1st and 4th, Trenchard, 2nd and 3rd, Per fess or and argent, on a saltire engrailed sable five molets pierced argent (Ashfordby)   In pretence: Argent three trees eradicated proper (   )
Crests: Dexter, A dexter arm embowed vested gules cuffed argent the hand proper holding a knife argent   Sinister, An ass's head proper gorged with a plain collar or charged with three roundels gules
Mantling: Gules and argent   Motto: Resurgam
For the Rev. John Ashfordby-Trenchard, who m. 2nd, 1834, Sarah Baker Brooks, of Kingham, and d. 10 Mar. 1838, aged 67. She d. 8 Dec. 1866, aged 73. (M.I.; B.L.G. 1937 ed.)

4. Dexter background black
Qly, 1st and 4th, Per pale, paly of six argent and sable, and azure, in sinister chief a crescent or for difference (Trenchard), 2nd and 3rd, Per fess or and argent, on a saltire engrailed sable five molets or (Ashfordby), impaling, Qly, 1st and 4th, Azure a wolf rampant or (Davies), 2nd and 3rd, Azure a chevron between three eagles' heads erased or (Saunders)
Crests: Dexter, A dexter arm embowed vested azure cuffed or the hand proper holding a knife argent   Sinister, An ass's head erased collared sable, the collar charged with three molets or   Mantling: Gules and argent   Motto: Nosce teipsum
For the Rev. John Trenchard Craven Ashfordby-Trenchard, who m. 1839, Mary Elizabeth Jane, only dau. of the Rev. Samuel Davies, of Northaw, and d. 10 Mar. 1851. (M.I.; B.L.G. 1937 ed.)

SWINDON, Holy Rood

1. Sinister background black
Argent on a chevron gules three towers argent, on a canton azure a

fleur-de-lys or (Vilett), impaling, Gules a chevron vair between three crescents argent (Goddard)
Cherub's head above shield
For Mary, dau. of Ambrose Goddard, who m. Thomas Vilett, and was bur. 30 Jan. 1760. (B.L.G. 2nd ed.; Record Office, Trowbridge)
(This hatchment was recorded in 1952, and is now in the Museum, Bath Road)

2. All black background
On a lozenge   Vilett, impaling, Or a chevron between three apples gules (Southby)
For Harriet Southby, who m. the Rev. Thomas Goddard Vilett (son of Thomas), and d. 12 Nov. 1836. (Sources, as 1.)
(This hatchment was recorded in 1952, but is now missing)

TOCKENHAM

1. Dexter background black
Qly of six, 1st and 6th, Argent a lion rampant tail erect and over the head sable, in chief the Badge of Ulster (Buxton), 2nd, Or two stags lodged gules (Buxton), 3rd, Or on a canton sable a tiger's head affronté erased or (Jacob), 4th, Per pale argent and sable a chevron between three talbots passant counterchanged, on a chief gules a leopard's face or (Gooch), 5th, Sable a chevron between three storks argent beaked and legged gules (Heron), impaling, Qly, 1st and 4th, Gules in chief two helmets argent garnished or and in base a garb or (Cholmeley), 2nd and 3rd, Azure on a chief argent three eagles displayed sable (Harrison)
Crest: A stag's head erased gules attired or   Mantling: Gules and argent   Motto: Grata sume manu
For Sir John Jacob Buxton, 2nd Bt., who m. 1825, Elizabeth, eldest dau. of Sir Montague Cholmeley, 1st Bt., of Easton Hall, Lincs, and d. 13 Oct. 1842. (B.P. 1875 ed.)

WESTBURY

1. All black background
Qly, 1st and 4th, Azure on a chevron between three eagles rising or six bars gules, on a chief or five lozenges azure (Lopes), 2nd and 3rd, In a landscape field a fountain, issuing therefrom a palm tree, all proper (Franco)
Baron's coronet   Crests: Dexter, A lion sejant or ermined sable gorged with a collar gemel gules the dexter paw resting on a lozenge azure   Sinister, A dexter arm embowed habited purpure, cuffed argent, the hand holding a palm branch vert

Motto: Quod tibi id alii   Supporters: On Roman fasces two pegasi sable winged and collared gemel or   All on a mantle gules and argent
For Henry Charles Lopes, 1st Baron Ludlow, who d. 25 Dec. 1899. (B.P. 1949 ed.)

2. **Dexter background black**
Azure a trefoil slipped ermine within an orle of eight molets argent (Phipps)   In pretence: Ermine a chief quarterly or and gules (Peckham)
Crest: A lion's gamb erased erect sable holding a molet argent
Mantling: Gules and argent
For Thomas Phipps, of Heywood House, who m. 1742, Sarah, dau. of Richard Peckham, and d. 1776, aged 68. (Burke's Commoners, Vol. 4.)

3. **All black background**
Qly, 1st and 4th, Phipps, 2nd and 3rd, Gules six lozenges conjoined in bend ermine (Hele)   In pretence: Qly, 1st and 4th, Argent a lion rampant sable between three trefoils slipped vert (Leckonby), 2nd and 3rd, Azure a lion rampant guardant or (Hothersall)
Crest: From the stump of a tree eradicated sable a trefoil ermine slipped and leaved vert   Mantling: Gules and argent   Motto: Virtute quies
For Thomas Henry Hele Phipps, who m. 1799, Mary, only dau. and heir of William Leckonby, and d. 8 Aug. 1841. (B.L.G. 5th ed.; Chetham Soc. Vol. 25, 188/9)

4. **Dexter background black**
Argent a chevron between three bears' heads erased sable (Ludlow)
In pretence: Argent three battleaxes sable (Gibbs)
Crest: A demi-bear sable   Mantling: Gules and argent   Motto: In coelo quies
For Abraham Ludlow, who m. 1799, Susanna, only child and heiress of Gaisford Gibbs, and d. 3 July 1822. (B.L.G. 5th ed.)

5. **All black background**
On a lozenge surmounted by a cherub's head
Argent a chevron between three bears' heads couped sable (Ludlow)
In pretence: Or three battleaxes sable (Gibbs)
For Susanna, widow of Abraham Ludlow, d. 3 Jan. 1841. (B.L.G. 5th ed.)

WILSFORD, nr Amesbury

1. **All black background**
Per fess argent and azure three chaplets counterchanged (Duke), impaling, Argent a chevron between three garbs sable (Blake)

Crest: A demi-griffin or holding a chaplet azure   Mantling: Gules and argent
For Robert Duke, of Lake, who m. Frances, dau. of Henry Blake, of Bristol, and d. 1749. (Colt Hoare, Hist. of Mod. Wilts, Underditch, p. 139)

2. **Dexter background black**
Duke, impaling, Sable a cross or between in dexter chief a chough argent beaked and legged gules, in sinister chief a text T, and in base two crescents argent (Rashleigh)
Crest and mantling: As 1.   Motto: Mors janua vitæ
For Robert Duke (son of 1.), who m. Jane (d. 1805), dau. of Jonathan Rashleigh, of Menabilly, Cornwall, and d. 28 Mar. 1793. (Sources, as 1.; Gents. Mag. 377)

WILTON

1. **Dexter background black**
Per pale gules and azure three lions rampant argent (Herbert), impaling, Qly, 1st and 4th, Qly argent and gules in the second and third quarters a fret or, over all on a bend sable three escallops argent (Spencer), 2nd and 3rd, Sable a lion rampant argent, on a canton argent a cross gules (Churchill)
Earl's coronet   Crest: A wyvern vert winged or   Mantling: Gules and argent   Motto: Ung je serviray   Supporters: Dexter, A panther guardant argent semy of roundels azure, gules, vert, sable and or, with flames issuant from mouth and ears proper   Sinister, A wyvern argent collared sable, the collar charged with three escallops argent and chained argent   No frame
For Henry, 10th Earl of Pembroke, who m. 1756, Elizabeth, dau. of Charles, 3rd Duke of Marlborough, and d. 26 Jan. 1794. (B.P. 1949 ed.)

2. **All black background**
A shield and an asymmetric lozenge   Dexter, shield, within the Garter, Per pale azure and gules three lions rampant argent (Herbert)
Sinister, lozenge, Herbert, impaling, Per bend argent and gules a fleur-de-lys between two roses in bend counterchanged, on a chief sable a chevron or charged with three bombs sable fired proper between three molets argent (Woronzow)
Countess's coronet   Mantle: Gules and ermine   Supporters: Dexter, as 1., but ducally gorged azure   Sinister, A lion rampant argent ducally gorged gules
For Catherine, only dau. of Simon, Count Woronzow, who m. 1808, as his 2nd wife, George Augustus, 11th Earl of Pembroke, and d. 27 Mar. 1856. (B.P. 1949 ed.)

3. Dexter background black

Herbert, as 2., impaling, Gules a lion rampant within a bordure engrailed or (Talbot)
Earl's coronet   Crest: A wyvern vert, underparts and under wing argent   Motto: Ung je serviray   Supporters: As 2.
For George Robert Charles, 13th Earl of Pembroke, who m. 1874, Gertrude Frances, dau. of Henry, 18th Earl of Shrewsbury, and d.s.p. 3 May 1895. (B.P. 1949 ed.)

WINTERBORNE BASSETT

1. All black background

Argent a chevron gules between three roundels azure (Baskerville), impaling, to the dexter, Per fess argent and sable in chief a sinister hand couped gules in base a salmon naiant argent (O'Neile), and to the sinister, Argent on a bend cotised gules three bezants (Bishop)
Crest: A wolf's head erased pierced through the mouth with a broken spear or embrued proper   Mantling: Gules and argent   Motto: Spero ut fidelis
For Thomas Baskerville, who m. 1st, Anne, only dau. of the Rev. James O'Neile, of Ballyshannon, co. Donegal, and 2nd, Jane, youngest dau. of Thomas Bishop, of Kinsale, and d.s.p. 4 May 1817. (B.L.G. 1937 ed.; Gents. Mag. 447)

2. Sinister background black

Qly of twenty-four, 1st and 24th, Baskerville, 2nd, Sable an eagle displayed or, on a chief azure bordered argent a chevron between two crescents in chief and a rose in base argent (Mynors), 3rd, Baskerville, 4th, Gules a fess countercompony argent and sable between six crosses patonce or (Boteler), 5th, Qly per fess indented gules and ermine a label of three points per pale or and sable (Rees), 6th, Gules a fess ermine in chief a label of six points or (Rees ap Griffith), 7th, Qly argent and azure on a bend sable three martlets or (Le Gros), 8th, Argent two lions passant azure (Paveley), 9th, Or a chevron azure between three lions' heads erased gules (Sollers), 10th, Argent a pale sable (Erskine), 11th, Gules a fess or between three escallops argent (Pychard), 12th, Argent on a bend gules three oval buckles or (Sapie), 13th, Argent a chevron between three martlets sable (Brenton), 14th, Gules a chevron between three escallops argent (Milborne), 15th, Gules fretty ermine (Eynsford), 16th, Argent a bend between six martlets gules (Furnival), 17th, Or a fret gules (Verdon), 18th, Argent a lion rampant sable crowned gules (Lovetot), 19th, Baskerville, a crescent or on the chevron for difference, 20th, Azure a bend cotised or between six cross crosslets fitchy argent (Blakett), 21st, Argent a griffin segreant reguardant sable (?Griffin), 22nd, Azure a fess between three chessrooks or (Bodenham), 23rd, Sable a horse's head erased between three gauntlets argent (Ap Gwillim)

Wiltshire

In pretence: Sable a chevron between three roundels argent each charged with a cock gules (Hancock)   Motto: Resurgam
For Anne, dau. and heiress of John Hancock of Marlborough, who m. 1818, as his 1st wife, Thomas Baskerville Mynors-Baskerville, of Rockley House, Wilts and Clyro Court, Radnor, and d. 13 June 1832. (B.L.G. 1937 ed.; M.I. at St Weonards; MS ped.)
(There is an identical hatchment in the parish church of St Weonard's, Herefordshire: her husband's hatchment is at Clyro, Radnorshire.)

SELECT BIBLIOGRAPHY

P. G. Summers, *How to read a Coat of Arms* (National Council of Social Service, 1967), 17-20.

P. G. Summers, *The Genealogists' Magazine*, vol. 12, No. 13 (1958), 443-446

T. D. S. Bayley and F. W. Steer, 'Painted Heraldic Panels', in *Antiquaries Journal*, vol. 35 (1955), 68-87.

L. B. Ellis, 'Royal Hatchments in City Churches', in *London and Middlesex Arch. Soc. Transactions* (New Series, vol. 10, 1948), 24-30 (contains extracts from a herald-painter's work-book relating to hatchments and 18th-century funerals).

C. A. Markham, 'Hatchments', in *Northampton & Oakham Architectural Soc. Proceedings*, vol. 20, Pt. 2 (1912), 673-687.

P. S. Spokes, 'Coats of Arms in Berkshire Churches', in *Berkshire Archaeological Journal*, vols. 35 to 45.

A. Schomberg, 'Church Heraldry of North Wiltshire', in *Wiltshire Archaeological Magazine*, vols. 23 to 25.

INDEX

Acland, Elizabeth, 138
Acland, Maria Palmer, 77
Addington, 16
Ailesbury, Charles, 1st Marquess of, 118
Ailesbury, Charles, 3rd Marquess of, 119
Ailesbury, Thomas, 1st Earl of, 118
Ainslie, Anne Penelope, 77
Albany, H.R.H. Prince Leopold, Duke of, 121, 126
Allen, Louisa, 36
Allen, Thomas, 48
Alston, Sir Rowland (6th Bt.), 14
Alston, Thomas, 14
Andrew, Elizabeth, 124
Annesley, Rev. Martin, 33
Anson, Sir William Reynell (3rd Bt.), 100
Antrobus, Sir Edmund (2nd Bt.), 117
Armistead, Elizabeth Bridget, 129
Ashe, Robert, 134
Ashe, Rev. Robert Martyn, 134
Ashfordby-Trenchard, Rev. John, 148
Ashfordby-Trenchard, Rev. John Trenchard Craven, 148
Astell, Elizabeth, 20
Astley, Francis Dugdale, 128
Astley, Sir John (2nd Bt.), 128
Astley, Sir John Dugdale (1st Bt.), 128
Astley, 128
Aston, Salisbury, 71
Atkyns, John Tracy, 108
Aufrere, Louisa, 46
Austen, 65
Austin, Edmund Stone, 94
Austin, 94
Awdry, Ambrose, 147
Awdry, Jane, 147
Ayliffe, Sir George, 121, 136

Badger, Sarah, 69
Baker, Edward, 144
Baker, Rev. Henry, 144
Barlow, 82
Barnard, Anne, 80, 81
Barney, Lydia, 94
Baron, Frances, 47
Barrett, Bryant, 35
Barwick, Newe, 55
Baskerville, Thomas, 152
Bateson, Elizabeth Honoria, 120
Bath, Thomas, 2nd Marquess of, 134
Batt, John, 145
Beard, Elizabeth Jessie, 9
Becher, 126
Beckford, Elizabeth, 72
Bedford, Francis Charles Hastings, 9th Duke of, 52
Bedford, Hastings William Sackville, 12th Duke of, 52
Bedford, John, 4th Duke of, 51
Bedford, William, 1st Duke of, 51
Belson, Mary, 35
Bennet, William Bathurst Pye, 122
Berkeley, Norborne (1st Baron Botetourt), 131
Bertie, Peregrine, 78
Bigg, 83
Bird, Catherine, 64
Biscoe, Mary, 12
Bishop, Jane, 152
Bisshopp, Catherine, 94
Blackall, Philippa, 145
Blackwell, Anne, 32
Blackwell, Mary, 32
Blake, Frances, 151
Blount, Rev. Henry Tichborne, 98
Blount, Joseph, 98
Blount, Lyster, 97
Blount, Michael, 97
Blount, Michael Henry Mary, 97
Boldero, Sophia, 50

Bolton, Lieut.-Gen. Sir Robert, 107
Botetourt, Norborne, 1st Baron, 131
Bouchier, Elizabeth, 95
Boulton, Matthew Robinson, 109
Bouverie-Pusey, Hon. Philip, 36
Bouverie-Pusey, Philip Francis, 37
Bowyer, Sir George (6th & 2nd Bt.), 38
Boyle, Hon. Arabella, 79
Boyle, Lady Juliana, 118
Boynton, Sarah, 93
Brandreth, Alice, 10
Brandreth, Humphrey, 10
Brant, James, 34
Breedon, Charles, 36
Breedon, Elizabeth, 38
Breedon, John, 36
Breedon, Rev. John Symonds, 35
Breedon, John Symonds, 36
Broadhead, Elizabeth, 83
Brodrick, Amelia, 147
Broke, Isabella Mary, 29
Bromhead, Frances, 11
Brooks, Sarah Baker, 148
Brown, Maria, 60
Browne, Henrietta, 107
Brownsword, Sarah, 16
Bruce, Charles (3rd Earl of Ailesbury), 119
Bruce, Louisa Caroline, 122
Brudenell, Lady Harriet Georgiana, 71
Brudenell-Bruce, Charles (1st Marquess of Ailesbury), 118
Brudenell-Bruce, Thomas (1st Earl of Ailesbury), 118
Bruges, Thomas, 138, 147
Brydges, Lady Anna Eliza, 77
Buccleuch, Henry, 3rd Duke of, 112
Buchanan, Sarah, 17
Buckingham & Chandos, Richard, 1st Duke of, 77
Buckinghamshire, Augustus Edward, 6th Earl of, 61
Buckinghamshire, George Robert, 5th Earl of, 61

Buckler, Mary, 128
Bullock, John, 16
Burgoyne, Frances, 18
Burrell, Margaret, 90
Burroughes, Anna Maria, 146
Burt, Mary, 146
Burton, Harriet, 61
Burton, James, 132
Burwell?, 50
Buxton, Sir John Jacob (2nd Bt.), 149
Byng, Hon. Georgiana Elizabeth, 51
Byng, Hon. Isabella Elisabeth, 134
Byng, 140

Caesar, Jane, 103
Calcraft, Gen. John, 139
Calley, Thomas, 122
Calverley, Catherine, 130
Cameron, Donald, 61
Campbell-Wyndham, Lieut.-Col. John, 143
Canning, Mary, 98
Capel, 49
Carrington, Robert, 1st Baron, 80, 81
Carrington, Robert John, 2nd Baron, 60
Carteret, Lady Sophia, 80
Cave, Penelope, 66
Cayley, Lucy Violet, 37
Chafin, Mary, 127
Chafin, Thomas, 138
Chafin, William, 138
Chamberlayne, Penelope, 96
Chelmsford, Frederick, 1st Viscount, 101
Chester, Mary, 47
Chetwode, Rev. George, 46
Chevall, 49
Child, Anne, 76
Cholmeley, Elizabeth, 149
Clarke, Mary, 91
Clarke, William Wiseman, 28
Clavering, Elizabeth, 79
Clayton, Sir William (1st Bt.), 66
Clayton, Sir William (4th Bt.), 67

Index

Clayton, William, 67
Clowes, Frances, 64
Cobham, Alexander, 38
Cockayne, Beatrice, 13
Cocks, Margaretta Sarah, 67
Coke, Elizabeth, 68
Collins, Charlotte, 136
Colquhoun, William, 9
Congreve, Ralph, 27
Congreve, Rev. Richard, 27
Congreve, William, 27
Cook, Ann, 35
Cooke, Martha, 148
Cooke, 135
Cooper, Elizabeth, 17
Cooper, Sarah Marianne, 132
Cooper, Sir William (5th Bt.), 124
Cooper, William Dodge Cooper, 17
Cope, Sir Charles (2nd Bt.), 94
Cotton, Alice, 19
Cottrell-Dormer, Sir Charles, 103
Cottrell-Dormer, Charles, 104
Cottrell-Dormer, Sir Clement, 104
Coussmaker, Sophia (Baroness de Clifford), 52
Coventry-Campion, Rev. John William, 19
Cramlington, Anne, 75
Creed, Elizabeth, 64
Cremorne, Thomas, 1st Viscount, 74
Cresswell, John Wentworth, 66
Cresswell, William Wentworth, 66
Crutchfield, William, 30
Cullum, 82
Cunliffe, Margaret Elizabeth, 65
Curzon, Assheton, 1st Viscount, 70
Curzon, George Augustus (2nd Earl Howe), 71
Curzon, Richard William (1st Earl Howe), 71
Cuthbert, Elizabeth, 15

Daly, Letitia, 134
Daniel, Charles Henry Olive, 103
Daniell, Jeffery, 141
Dashwood, Sir George (4th Bt.), 96
Dashwood, Sir George Henry (5th Bt.), 83
Dashwood, Sir Henry Watkin (3rd Bt.), 96
Dashwood, Sir James (2nd Bt.), 96
Dashwood, Sir Robert (1st Bt.), 96
Dashwood, Robert, 95
Davers, Frederica Louisa, 8
Davies, Mary Elizabeth Jane, 148
Dawson, Thomas (1st Viscount Cremorne), 74
Delap, James Bogle, 66
Deloraine, Henry, 1st Earl of, 105
Dickson, Col. A., 63
Digby, Maria, 129
Digby, 75
Dillon, Charles, 12th Viscount, 106
Dillon, Henry Augustus, 13th Viscount, 107
Dixon, Susanna, 7
Dodwell, Mary, 109
Donnelly, Frances Mary, 30
Douglas, Anne Hammond, 38
Douglas-Hamilton, Lady Susan, 108
Dowdeswell, Anne, 95
Drew, Caroline, 133
Duke, Robert, 151
Duncan, 63
Dunch, Mary, 108
Duncombe, Anne, 105
Duncombe, Elizabeth, 56
Duncombe, Francis, 47
Dunkerron, James, Viscount, 79
Du Pré, Sophia, 49
Durnford, Gertrude, 14
Dutton, 82

Eardley, Hon. Maria Marow, 91
Eardley-Twisleton-Fiennes, Gregory William (14th Baron Saye and Sele), 91, 92
Eardley-Twisleton-Fiennes, William Thomas (15th Baron Saye and Sele), 92
East, Mary, 67
Edmeades, Mary Anne, 130
Egerton, Elizabeth, 145

Egremont, Maria Isabella, 61
Ellis, Charlotte, 10
Ellison, George, 68
Ellison, Thomas, 68
Englefield, Martha, 97
Ernle, Elizabeth, 125
Ernle, Rachel, 141
Ernle, 125
Errington, Frances, 106
Esdaile, Louisa, 63
Evans, Anne, 33
Everett, 135
Eyre, Elizabeth, 146
Eyre, John, 146
Eyre, 146

Farrer, William Frederick, 70
Farrer-Hillersdon, Denis, 9
Farrer-Hillersdon, Elizabeth, 9
Farrer-Hillersdon, Sarah, 5
Feilding, Adm. Charles, 134
Fermor, Henry, 106
Fermor, Lady Juliana, 73
Fermor, Lady Louisa, 67
Fermor, William, 106
Fettiplace, Anne, 92
Fiennes, Lawrence (5th Viscount Saye & Sele), 90
Fiennes, Mary, 90
Fiennes, Hon. Richard, 90
Fiennes, William (3rd Viscount Saye & Sele), 90
Finch, Lady Heneage, 8
Fisher, Rt. Hon. Albert Laurence, 102
Fitzmaurice, Hon. Thomas, 80
Fitzpatrick, Lady Louisa, 80
Fletcher, Capt. Francis Charteris, 37
Flower, Hon. Elizabeth, 131
Foley, Very Rev. Robert, 95
Forbes, Isabella, 74
Forester, Hon. Elizabeth Catherine, 60
Fox, Charles James, 129
Fox, Henry (1st Baron Holland), 129
Fox-Strangways, Lady Elizabeth Theresa, 134

Fox-Strangways, Henry Thomas (2nd Earl of Ilchester), 129
Francis, Rev. Charles, 139
Frankland-Russell, Sir Robert (7th Bt.), 53
Fraser, Henry, 82
Fraser, Jean Helen, 119
Freame, Philadelphia Hannah, 74
Freke, Mary, 138
Fromow, Ann Ruth, 34
Fuller, Benjamin, 55
Fuller, John, 144
Fuller, John Stratton, 56

Gale, Penelope, 33
Gale, Sarah, 138, 147
Gardner, Anne, 91
Gaskell, Capt. William, 50
Gayer, Elizabeth, 74
Geast, Anne, 128
Gee, Sarah, 9
Gee, 83
Gerrard, Sarah, 58
Gibbard, Susannah, 13
Gibbs, Susanna, 150
Giffard, Maria Catherine, 30
Gladstone, John Neilson, 120
Goddard, Mary, 149
Goddard, 140
Godin, Jane, 6
Gomm, Field Marshal Sir William, 74
Goodall, Rev. William, 57
Gooding, 144
Gordon, Charlotte, 110
Gosfright, Frances, 18
Gosling, Robert, 64
Gosling, William, 65
Graeme, Catherine, 60
Graham, Mary Helen, 96
Green, 82
Greenhill-Russell, Sir Robert (1st Bt.), 53
Grenville, Richard (1st Duke of Buckingham & Chandos), 77
Grosvenor, Dorothy, 71
Grosvenor, Sherrington, 65

Index

Grove, Charles, 138
Grove, Elizabeth, 138
Grove, Hugh, 127
Grove, John, 119, 127
Grove, Rev. Thomas, 139
Grove, Thomas, 119
Grove, Sir Thomas Fraser (1st Bt.), 120
Grove, Rev. William, 139
Grove, William Chafin, 138
Guy, Hannah, 147

Halhed, Ellen Frances, 34
Halsey, Edmund, 76
Hamilton, Col. Walter, 75
Hammet, Sir Benjamin, 63
Hammet, Elizabeth, 62
Hampden, John, 3rd Viscount, 61
Hampden, Thomas, 2nd Viscount, 60
Hanbury, Mary, 33, 36
Hancock, Anne, 153
Hanham, Eleanor, 119
Hanmer, Ann Eleanora Isabella, 78
Hanmer, Esther, 70
Harcourt, Edward William, 99
Harcourt, George Simon, 2nd Earl, 98
Hare, Sir Robert, 49
Harter, Rev. George Gardner, 9
Hartley, Winchcombe Henry, 32
Hartley, Rev. Winchcombe Henry Howard, 32
Harvey, Dorothy, 20
Harvey, John, 7, 13, 17
Haviland, Gen. William, 71
Hawes, Rev. John, 146
Hawes, Margaret Jane, 143
Hawkes, Maria Elizabeth, 59
Hawkins, Mary, 39
Hawley, Catherine Toovey, 36
Hayter, William, 145
Hearst, Sarah, 142
Henshaw, Philip, 39
Hepburn, 81
Herbert, Lady Emily Frances Theresa, 37

Herbert, George Augustus (11th Earl of Pembroke), 151
Herbert, George Robert Charles (13th Earl of Pembroke), 152
Herbert, Henry (10th Earl of Pembroke), 151
Herbert, Vere Catherine Louisa, 61
Hervey, Barbara, 132
Hesketh, Frances, 73
Heylin, Elizabeth, 104
Heywood, Lucy, 30
Hibbert, Thomas, 50
Hibbert, 50
Hicks, John, 46
Higginson, John, 68, 69
Hill, Hon. Henrietta Maria, 118
Hillier, Harriet, 66
Hippisley, John, 148
Hoare, Henry Arthur, 78
Hoare, Henry Charles, 77
Hoare, Sir Henry Hugh (3rd Bt.), 77
Hoare, Susanna, 118
Hobart, Augustus Edward (6th Earl of Buckinghamshire), 61
Hobart, George Robert (5th Earl of Buckinghamshire), 61
Holland, Georgiana Caroline, Baroness, 129
Holland, Henry, 1st Baron, 129
Holroyd, Lady Susan Harriet, 99
Holt, Ann, 123
Horlock, Susanna Jemima, 47
Hornby, Rev. James John, 58
Houghton, Elizabeth, 64
Howard, Field Marshal Sir George, 72
Howard, Mary, 105
Howard-Vyse, Richard Henry, 73
Howard-Vyse, Richard William Howard, 73
Howe, George Augustus, 2nd Earl, 71
Howe, Richard William, 1st Earl, 71
Huddleston, 111
Hudson, Charlotte, 81
Hughes, Mary, 107
Hulme, Rev. George, 38
Hussey, Eleanor, 6

Ilchester, Henry Thomas, 2nd Earl
  of, 129
Inglis, Sir Hugh (1st Bt.), 12
Inglis, Hugh, 11
Inglis, Mary Louisa, 12
Inglis, Sir Robert Harry (2nd Bt.), 12
Inglis, Stephena Anne, 12
Isham, Edward, 100

Jackson, Sarah, 48
Jacob, John, 131
Jacob, 132
James, Rev. Montague Rhodes, 58
James, William, 29
Jekyll, Anne, 59
Jennens, Elizabeth, 40
Johnson, Ann, 66
Johnson, Catherine, 11
Jolliffe, Hon. Julia Agnes, 73
Jones, Fanny Richarda, 70
Jones, Henry, 92
Jones, Martha, 27
Jones, Rev. William, 48
Joye, Anne, 33

Kaye, John, 58
Keck, Anthony Tracy, 108
Keck, Elizabeth Anne, 122
Keck, Francis, 108
Keck, John, 108
Keck, Thomas Tracy, 109
Kemeys-Tynte, Anne, 124
Kenrick, Martha, 66
Kenton, 143
Keppel, Lady Elizabeth, 51
Kerr, Elizabeth, 28
Kingston, Harriet Wilson, 54
Kirkman, Hannah, 48

Lake, Francis, 2nd Viscount, 45
Lane, Julia Lucy, 78
Langford, Anne, 55
Lansdowne, William, 1st Marquess
  of, 80
Latour, Georgiana, 60
Lawson-Johnston, George (1st
  Baron Luke), 14

Lawton, Ann, 19
Leckonby, Mary, 150
Lee, Caroline, 71
Leeds, George Godolphin, 8th Duke
  of, 75
Legge, Rt. Rev. Hon. Edward, 100
Legh, Elizabeth, 123
Leighton, Anne, 136
Leighton, Francis Knyvett, 100
Lennox, Georgiana Caroline (Baroness Holland), 129
Lenthall, Edmund Henry, 30
Lenthall, Edmund Kyffin, 29
Lenthall, Philip John, 29
Lenthall, Walter Ellison, 30
Lenthall, William, 92
Leveson-Gower, Lady Anne, 99
Leveson-Gower, Lady Gertrude, 51
Leveson-Gower, Gen. John, 29
Light, Hester Eleanor, 109
Lindsay, Anne, 117
Lindsay, Katharine, 108
Littledale, Mary, 7
Livesay, Gen. John, 15
Lloyd, Maria Eliza Catherina, 67
Long, Anne, 125
Long, Eleanor, 145
Long, Philippa, 119
Long, Walter, 145
Long, Sir William, 11
Longuet, Maria, 15
Lopes, Henry Charles (1st Baron
  Ludlow), 150
Lovell, Peter Harvey, 137
Lowndes, Charles, 54
Lowndes, Isabella, 89
Lowndes, William, 54
Lowndes, William Selby, 78
Lowndes-Stone, William Francis, 90
Lowth, Mary, 93
Lowther, Rev. Chambre Brabazon
  Ponsonby, 140
Ludlow, Abraham, 150
Ludlow, Henry Charles, 1st Baron,
  150
Luke, George, 1st Baron, 14
Luke, 8

Index

Mabbott, Frances, 46
Marjoribanks, Edward, 60
Martin-Atkins, Atkins Edwin, 35
Martin-Atkins, Edwin, 34
Martyn, Thermuthis, 134
Mason, Mary Harriet, 54
May, Jane, 35
May, Louisa, 137
Mellish, Catherine, 58
Meredith, Anna Margaretta, 71
Merewether, 137
Meux, Sir Henry (2nd Bt.), 122
Michell, Eleanor, 139
Milne, 63
Milnes, Anne Beckingham, 16
Minshull, George Rowland, 45
Molloy, Charles, 47
Molloy, Mary, 48
Monoux, Sir Humphrey (2nd Bt.), 19
Monoux, Sir Humphrey (4th Bt.), 21
Monoux, Humphrey, 20
Monoux, Lewis, 20
Monoux, Sir Philip (3rd Bt.), 20
Monoux, Sir Philip (5th Bt.), 21
Monoux, Sir Philip (6th Bt.), 21
Monoux, Rev. Sir Philip (7th Bt.), 21
Montagu, Lady Elizabeth, 112
Montefiore, Louisa, 45
Moore, Susanna Jane, 63
Mordaunt, Charles (5th Earl of Peterborough), 126
Morgan, George, 46
Morland, Mary Ann, 110
Mornington, William, 5th Earl of, 127
Morris, Vice-Adm. Sir James Nicoll, 67
Mortimer, Charles, 101
Mure, Katherine, 47
Murray, Louisa Anne, 53
Mynors-Baskerville, Thomas, 153

Naish, Anne, 127
Neale, John Alexander, 103
Neeld, Joseph, 147
Newman, Jane, 39
Niblett, Stephen, 99
Nixon, Augusta Eliza, 69
Norton, Rev. James, 89
Nourse, Elizabeth Johanna, 110
Nourse, Hester, 140
Nourse, John, 110

O'Grady, Katherine Grace, 120
O'Grady, Mary Theresa, 129
Oliver, Anna Elizabeth, 46
O'Loghlin, Gen. Terence, 49
O'Neile, Anne, 152
Ongley, Robert, 1st Baron, 18
Ongley, Robert, 2nd Baron, 18
Onslow, Anne, 45
Orkney, Mary, Countess of, 80
Orlebar, Cooper, 14
Orlebar, John, 15
Orlebar, Richard, 15
Orlebar, Robert Charles, 10
Orlebar, Robert Shipton, 10
Osborn, Sir George (4th Bt.), 8
Osborn, Sir John (5th Bt.), 8
Osborne, George Godolphin (8th Duke of Leeds), 75
Osborne, Lydia Mary, 54

Page, Sarah, 128
Palliser, Adm. Sir Hugh (1st Bt.), 49
Palmer, Sir Charles Harcourt (6th Bt.), 57
Palmer, Rev. Henry, 58
Paris, Harriet Mary, 7
Pattison, Mark, 102
Payne, Augusta, 21
Paynter, Charles Paulet Camborne, 133
Paynter, George William, 133
Pearse, Sophia, 7
Peckham, Sarah, 150
Peers, Charles, 93
Pembroke, George Augustus, 11th Earl of, 151
Pembroke, George Robert Charles, 13th Earl of, 152

Pembroke, Henry, 10th Earl of, 151
Penn, Granville, 74
Penn, John, 74
Penn, Sophia, 74
Penn, Thomas, 73
Penruddocke, Arundel, 142
Peperell, Mary, 27
Peterborough, Charles, 5th Earl of, 126
Petre, Catherine, 97
Petre, Hon. Elizabeth Anne Mary, 97
Petty, Henry (1st Earl of Shelburne), 79
Petty, James (Viscount Dunkerron), 79
Petty, William (1st Marquess of Lansdowne), 80
Phillips, John, 93
Phipps, Hon. Henrietta Maria, 106
Phipps, Jane, 144
Phipps, Thomas, 150
Phipps, Thomas Henry Hele, 150
Pigot, Anne Glover, 61
Pigot, Adm. Hugh, 75
Pilfold, Charlotte, 119
Pinfold, Ann, 77
Plaistowe, 65
Pleydell-Bouverie, Hon. Duncombe, 137
Plowden, Mary, 31
Pocock, Sir Isaac, 33
Pocock, Nicholas, 33
Pole-Tylney-Long-Wellesley, William (5th Earl of Mornington), 127
Pollen, Sir John (1st Bt.), 123
Pomeroy, Henry William, 48
Poole, Mary, 108
Poore, Sir John Methuen (1st Bt.), 142
Popham, Gen. Edward William Leyborne, 124
Powell, Francis, 146
Powney, Elizabeth, 14
Poynder, Thomas, 132
Poynder, Thomas Henry Allen, 130
Priestley, George, 48
Primrose, Archibald (5th Earl of Rosebery), 70

Prynce, Mary, 128
Pryse, Elizabeth, 36
Pusey, Clara, 37
Pusey, Philip, 37
Pye, Henry, 34

Radcliffe, Anthony, 47
Radford, John, 101
Rashleigh, Jane, 151
Rawdon, Lady Anne, 118
Rawdon, Elizabeth Anne, 52
Raymond, Mabel, 39
Raynesford, Elizabeth, 14
Reade, Dorothea, 95
Rich, Sir George (6th Bt.), 31
Ricketts, Elizabeth Sophia, 46
Riddell, Elizabeth, 21
Risley, Henry, 56
Risley, Paul, 56
Risley, Risley, 56
Robinson, Rev. Sir John (1st Bt.), 62
Robinson, Margaret, 104
Robinson, Sarah Gore, 13
Rogier, Marie, 106
Rolls, Jane, 49
Rolt, Mary, 15
Rosebery, Archibald, 5th Earl of, 7
Rothschild, Sir Anthony (1st Bt.), 48
Rothschild, Hon. Hannah, 70
Rouse-Boughton, Louisa, 6
Rowden, Rev. Edward, 131
Rowles, Elizabeth, 34
Rowley, Marianne Sarah, 96
Russell, Frances, 75
Russell, Francis (Marquess of Tavistock), 51
Russell, Francis Charles Hastings (9th Duke of Bedford), 52
Russell, Gen. Lord George William, 52
Russell, Hastings William Sackville (12th Duke of Bedford), 52
Russell, John (4th Duke of Bedford), 51
Russell, Lord John, 51
Russell, Commander John, 52

Index

Russell, William (1st Duke of Bedford), 51
Russell, Lord William, 19, 52

Sackville, Lady Elizabeth, 52
St John, Anne, 121, 136
St John, Hon. Edith Laura, 14
St John, Frederick, 3rd Viscount, 135
St John, George Richard, 4th Viscount, 136
St John, Sir John (1st Bt.), 136
St John, John, 11th Baron, 5
St John, St Andrew, 13th Baron, 6
St John, St Andrew Beauchamp, 14th Baron, 6
St John, Walter, 136
St John, Hon. William Henry Beauchamp, 5
St Paul, Horace, 111
Sambrook, Elizabeth, 21
Saunders, Sir Thomas, 49
Savage, Elizabeth, 27
Savage, Mary, 20
Saye & Sele, Fiennes, 11th Baron, 91
Saye & Sele, Gregory William, 14th Baron, 91, 92
Saye & Sele, John, 12th Baron, 91
Saye & Sele, Lawrence, 5th Viscount, 90
Saye & Sele, Thomas, 13th Baron, 91
Saye & Sele, William, 15th Baron, 92
Saye & Sele, William, 3rd Viscount, 90
Sayer, Vice-Adm. James, 105
Schomberg, Isaac, 147
Scott, Henry (3rd Duke of Buccleuch), 112
Scott, Henry (1st Earl of Deloraine), 105
Scott-Murray, Charles, 69
Scrope, Emma, 124
Selman, Sarah, 49
Sewell, James Edward, 102
Shales, Anne, 54
Shawe, Frances Anne, 93
Shelburne, Henry, 1st Earl of, 79
Sheldon, Frances, 106
Sherard, Lady Lucy, 36
Shipton, Charlotte, 10
Shrapnel, Lieut.-Gen. Henry 121
Shrimpton, 81
Silcock, Sarah, 13
Simond, Susannah Louisa, 5
Skeate, Anne, 135
Skottowe, Coulson, 55
Skrine, Sarah, 139
Slade, Anne Eliza, 142
Slade, Charlotte, 38
Small, Alexander, 56
Smith, Elizabeth, 68
Smith, Emma Jemima Barbara, 10
Smith, Frances Ann, 7
Smith, Joseph, 94, 95
Smith, Mary, 131
Smith, Robert (1st Baron Carrington), 80, 81
Smith, Robert John (2nd Baron Carrington), 60
Smyth, Sir William, 19
Sneyd, Lewis, 100
Sneyd, Sarah, 68
Southby, Catherine, 141
Southby, Charity Anne, 123
Southby, Harriet, 149
Southby, John, 28
Southby, Mary, 123
Southby, Richard, 39, 123
Southby, Richard Duke, 123
Southby, Sarah, 29
Spencer, Lady Diana, 135
Spencer, Lady Elizabeth, 151
Spencer, Elizabeth, 96
Spencer, Rev. Francis Charles, 110
Spencer, Mary Anne, 62
Spooner, Charles, 146
Spooner, Dr William Archibald, 102
Stapleton, Sir William (3rd Bt.), 75
Stawell, Hon. Charlotte, 27
Stewart, Harriette Emma Arundel, 75
Still, Richard, 139
Stone, 94

Stratton, Charlotte, 55
Stratton, George, 109
Strickland, Caroline, 90
Strickland, Frances Elizabeth, 104
Strickland, Mary Eugenia, 97
Strickland, Walter, 93
Sturt, Harriet Mary, 71
Sumner, Benedict Humphrey, 101
Sutton, Martha, 55
Swabey, Maurice, 64

Talbot, Lady Gertrude Frances, 152
Tatham, Edward, 101
Tavistock, Francis, Marquess of, 51
Taylor, Elizabeth Juliana, 56
Taylor, 105
Thesiger, Frederick (1st Viscount Chelmsford), 101
Thomas, Mary, 144
Thompson, James, 101
Thomson, George Poulett, 124
Thornton, Claude George, 7
Thornton, Godfrey, 6, 7
Thornton, Stephen, 7
Thoyts, William, 39
Throckmorton, Charles, 31
Throckmorton, Sir John Courtenay (5th Bt.), 30
Throckmorton, Sir Robert (4th Bt.), 30
Throckmorton, Robert Charles, 31
Thynne, Thomas (2nd Marquess of Bath), 134
Tollemache, Maria Elizabeth, 118
Tracy, John, 7th Viscount, 100
Tradescant, John, 103
Trenchard, Frances, 148
Trevor, Robert, 17
Trevor, Tudor, 40
Tufnell, Anna Louisa, 63
Turner, Elizabeth, 91
Turner, Sir John Crichloe, 75
Turner, 81
Twisleton, Fiennes (11th Baron Saye & Sele), 91
Twisleton, John (12th Baron Saye & Sele), 91

Twisleton, Thomas (13th Baron Saye & Sele), 91

Upton, Florence Ann, 104
Upton-Cottrell-Dormer, Clement, 104

Vanhattem, Sir John, 57
Vanhattem, Rebecca, 57
Vassall, Mary, 13
Venables, William, 34
Vernon, Hon. Elizabeth, 98
Vernon-Harcourt, Rt. Hon. & Most Rev. Edward, 99
Vilett, Thomas, 149
Vilett, Rev. Thomas Goddard, 149
Villiers, Lady Charlotte Anne, 19, 51

Wade-Gery, William Hugh, 16
Waldeck & Pyrmont, H.S.H. Princess Helen of, 121, 126
Walpole, Richard, 62
Wankford, Dorothy, 78
Ward, Charles, 82
Warde, Mary, 67
Warneford, Col. Francis, 130
Warneford, Francis, 131
Warneford, Harriet Elizabeth, 131
Warren, Isabella, 34
Warriner, Gifford, 125
Warriner, 125
Watkin, Rev. John Burton, 132
Watson, William, 33
Watts, Edward, 61
Watts, Elizabeth, 32
Webb, Lieut.-Gen. John Richmond, 135
Webb, 120
Welby, Selina, 20
Welch, Isabella, 81
Welles, Ann, 82
Welles, Charlotte, 82
Welles, Samuel, 81, 82
Wentworth, Lady Lucy, 72
Western, Frances, 93
Weston, Anne, 111

Index

Westwood, Thomas, 82
Wethered, Thomas, 69
Wetherell, Sir Charles, 131
Wetherell, Elizabeth, 131
Weyland, John, 110
Weyland, Richard, 110
Wheate, 50
Wheble, Lucy Catherine, 97
Whitaker, Ann, 56
Whitchurch, 143
Whitfield, Elizabeth, 99
Whitwell, Louisa, 52
Wilde, Mary, 30
Wilkinson, Elizabeth, 46
Wilkinson, Mary Anne, 109
Willes, Charlotte, 137
Williams, Rev. Sir Gilbert (5th Bt.), 78
Williams, Mary, 61
Williamson, Lieut. Gen. Sir Adam, 117
Williamson, Mary, 17
Willoughby, Hon. Charlotte Augusta Annabella, 60

Willoughby, Sir Henry Pollard (3rd Bt.), 98
Willoughby, Sir John Pollard (4th Bt.), 59
Wilson, Mary, 12
Wix, Mary, 132
Wodehouse, Lucy, 20
Wood, Rev. James, 11
Woolhouse, 75
Woronzow, Catherine, 151
Wrighte, Anne, 59
Wrighte, George, 59
Wrottesley, Frances, 75
Wykeham, William Richard, 107
Wynch, Florentina, 62
Wyndham, Caroline Frances, 143
Wyndham, Henry, 142
Wyndham, Wadham, 142

Yonge, Mary Josephine, 133
Young, Sir William Lawrence (3rd Bt.), 63